A VULTURE LANDSCAPE

A VULTURE
LANDSCAPE

TWELVE MONTHS IN EXTREMADURA

IAN PARSONS

Whittles Publishing

Published by
Whittles Publishing Ltd.,
Dunbeath,
Caithness, KW6 6EG,
Scotland, UK

www.whittlespublishing.com

© 2020 Ian Parsons

ISBN 978-184995-457-0

Printed by Cambrian Printers

For Jo and for Kate,
Y Por Los Buitres.

CONTENTS

ACKNOWLEDGEMENTS IX

APRIL 3

MAY 12

JUNE 23

JULY 32

AUGUST 43

SEPTEMBER 55

OCTOBER 65

NOVEMBER 75

DECEMBER 85

JANUARY 96

FEBRUARY 108

MARCH 119

APPENDICES 131

ACKNOWLEDGEMENTS

I would like to thank all the vulture workers and conservationists that are doing so much to not only safeguard our vulture populations, but to increase them. There are two organisations that I would like to thank in particular: the Vulture Conservation Foundation (VCF), who do a tremendous amount of work for our vultures. The fantastic projects in Europe I have mentioned and referenced in this book are largely down to them and their tireless work. I would also like to thank SEO (the Spanish Ornithological Society), who do so much to protect and promote the wonderful birds in the Vulture Landscape. The skies would be much emptier places without them.

I would like to thank Matt Merritt, my editor at *Bird Watching* magazine who, many years ago, published an article I had written on the Azure-winged Magpie and, in doing so, set me off on my writing journey. Thanks go to Mark Avery who has allowed me to write blogs for his excellent website, helping me develop my writing style in the process. Thanks must also go to Keith Whittles and the staff at Whittles Publishing for their support in bringing this book to fruition.

In Spain, I would like to thank Helios Dalmau for his friendship, company, chats and that Bonelli's Eagle! Thanks must also go to Santi and Javi for making us (and the clients) always feel welcome whenever we are in the Vulture Landscape. Finally, *gracias a todos los Extremeños*, the keepers of the Vulture Landscape.

My wife Jo has been wonderfully supportive; without her I couldn't do what I do. My daughter Kate is an inspiration, and my parents, who allowed me to grow up experiencing the wonders of nature in my own way.

A Griffon Vulture in flight above the vulture landscape.

INTRODUCTION

Birds of prey, or raptors as they are known, are a group of birds that always fascinate. For many people it is the powerful eagles that grab their attention; for others it is the falcons, all speed and glamour. But for me, it is the somewhat less glamorous members of the raptor tribe, the vultures.

Vultures are brilliant birds; birds that first captured my imagination as a child watching wildlife documentaries as these huge birds swarmed over large mammal carcasses on the African savannah. I can still remember seeing my first real-life one, even though it was a quarter of a century ago – an indelible memory of a Griffon Vulture drifting high up in the blue sky of a Spanish spring. I was instantly hooked.

Vultures are found all around the globe, including here in Europe where four species breed. This book is about the vultures that live, breed and feed in one of the best birdwatching areas of the continent – Extremadura in central Spain. It is a vulture landscape in the truest sense of the word. Vultures are a vital part of many of southern Europe's ecosystems. They share this landscape (and skyscape) with a vast community of other species, many of which also appear in the pages that follow. This book follows the vultures through a year of their lives, giving you a view into their world, allowing you to get to know them, their habits, their ecology and the threats they face.

The modern world has brought with it many pressures on our wildlife, and vultures are sadly no exception to this. Of the twenty-three species found across the world, half are either Endangered or Critically Endangered. This book looks at some of the reasons behind this worrying statistic as well as touching on some of the conservation successes of the last few decades, successes that have returned these majestic birds to many of their old European haunts.

To watch vultures circling over the plains, to gaze at a huge bird as it effortlessly glides through the air above the oaks of the dehesa, is an exhilarating expcrience that we should all have. I hope this book not only introduces you to their world, but also spurs you on to visit it.

APRIL

These are not the proverbial early birds. It has been several hours since the sun broke through the eastern horizon, yet still they wait in this artificial hole in the landscape. All other life seems busy; they do not. The soap opera lives of the Spanish Sparrows and Spotless Starlings play out around them. A pair of Rock Buntings, unobtrusively tied to the treadmill of parentage, provide a conveyor belt supply of food to their chicks hidden expertly in a fold of the granite just a few feet below. The tumbling, radio-static interrupted song of a Black Redstart mingles with the flute concerto of a Blue Rock Thrush, whilst the seemingly endless backing track of 'hoo-poe-poe' onomatopoeically pervades all. But these happenings, these sounds, are of no consequence to these leviathans of the avian world. The reverberating song of the Hoopoe bouncing off the rock, no matter how beautiful it sounds to me, is an unheard irrelevance in their world.

It is no coincidence that the one area of rock within this vastness of rock where the Griffon Vultures are encamped is the only place where the warmth-giving light of the morning sun now envelops everything. Their affinity to this narrow band in the wide spectrum of rock available is told by the rich hue of guano-fed colour that saturates the rock below. The blasted, scarred angular faces and ledges reflect the warmth and drive the motion of the air. It is for this that the Griffons await. They have, it seems to me, an unerring ability to read the air, to feel it, to sense its movement, its lift, its buoyancy. They can read the air, but we are illiterate.

They may, in our anthropocentric view of life, appear idle as they sit motionless on the ledge in the morning sun, but the reality is that they are ruthlessly efficient. This pause before action is a deliberate ploy that our own high-energy consuming existence struggles to comprehend. One bird on the edge of the main body of birds, probably a first-year judging by the underwing pattern, decides to wait no longer and off it steps to test the air. But this bird is premature, the lift isn't there yet and after a couple of laboured circles it comes back clumsily to the ledge, the echo of its wing beats rolling across the water to where I stand. The more experienced and dominant birds gathered in the prime spot ignore this impatience; the youngster will learn that the trait of impatience is one only to be used when feeding.

I am standing at one end of a large, long hole, quarried out of the earth many decades ago. The hard rock that lies just inches below the thin, scrubby soils of this area was judged ideal to be ripped out of the ground and used in the construction of a vast concrete dam that now tames the once wild and reckless river Tajo that knife slashes its way across the geography of Extremadura. In an ironic twist, the wildness of the river has gone, leaving only a benign vestige of what it once was. But the hole made to create the taming dam has since gone wild itself, long abandoned by man and flooded by impenetrable depths of water. This quarry has become an untamed place, a place where vultures reign.

The narrowed perspective of being in the quarry makes it look as if the face on which these magnificent birds wait is only a few tens of metres away; in fact, it is over three-hundred metres from me – the scale dwarfs everything and tricks the eye. It is in situations like this that you appreciate the camouflage of the Griffon. Without knowing they were there, you simply wouldn't see them. I watch, waiting for the birds. It doesn't always happen like this, but I have watched this colony on many mornings, over many years, and have watched this play out many times. From behind me a Black Kite enters the quarry, riding the unseen turbulent air that the narrow rock-lined entrance creates. It is wary of my figure, giving me a wide berth as it passes into the open space of this large hole. Once in, it glides with ease over the lower tier of ledges, scattering a previously unseen group of Linnets and burning yellow Serins from their feeding amongst the ungrazed grasses that tenuously carpet some of the ledges. A male Common Kestrel screams off his lookout rock, an incandescent dive-bombing rage. The kite has strayed too close to the falcon's nest and has to take avoiding action to evade the darting attack. It twists away from the face, losing its graceful composure and has to flap those long wings as it spirals away from the rock and out over the black water of the quarry. It turns back to ride the uplift, gliding close once more along the face, surfing the warmth. The tenacious small falcon still screams, but more for show now that the kite has altered its course.

The vultures witness all of this. It might be pure imagination on my part, but I believe they are watching this long-winged raptor, watching how it rides the air, judging whether it is time. The kite, on gliding wings, completes a circuit of the quarry, drifting right past the mass of vultures as it does so, not once since its spat with the small tenacious falcon has it flapped those long wings. It is surely time.

They begin to step off. We would typically describe this motion as stepping in to the void, but a void means an empty space and to a vulture the air is not an empty space. They don't step off into a void; they step off into a living, moving entity that can be ridden and exploited. An initial drop of height as they unfurl their huge broad wings is swiftly reversed as these feathered sails catch the updraft of warmth and, without a flap, they are away, floating in a sea of air. This is what they have been waiting for, the chance to get airborne without having to expend energy. One after another they step off the ledge, circling the openness, gaining height without flapping or effort. The first of the birds to do so has already gained enough height to be clear of the confining walls of the quarry. Its eyes are now scanning the vast open landscape before it, they are seeing so many things, but they are also studying the air, select-ing the most efficient path to follow to continue to gain height. How they judge this, how they know where to fly in this vast three-dimensional world comes down to their ability to read it. The first one is away, heading slightly to my left as I watch it come nearer and nearer before passing above me. I am transfixed. I have seen this so often, but every time I see it, the sense of awe is like the first. I turn back to watch the second, third, fourth, fifth… all come past, all following the exact same path that to me is completely unmarked and untraceable. The huge birds with their monumental wingspans pass right by me. I am spellbound; they are majestically indifferent.

I grew up on the Sunday evening nature programmes that seemed to be a fixture of my childhood television experience. I enjoyed them immensely and lapped up every little detail, every nugget of information, even though they signified that the freedom of the weekend was coming to an end and the grind of school was returning. I am

Vultures are huge birds, close encounters with them can leave you utterly spellbound.

sure there were other areas featured, but the impression they left in my mind is one of African savannah, seemingly endless programmes about this vast, wild grass and scrub land. Whether the focal point was wildebeest, lions or graceful, jumping gazelles, at some point in the programme a carcass would feature and, when it did, so did huge, bickering, almost reptilian-looking birds. Vultures.

Vultures were an African experience in my mind. I didn't realise they were found elsewhere; I certainly didn't realise they could be found in Europe. If someone had told me that less than a two-hour flight from where I sat watching the pictures of vultures squabbling and bickering over a dead zebra, I could actually see vultures in the wild, I simply wouldn't have believed them. That can be the problem with television sometimes– as much as it can open your eyes it can also stop you looking. Southern Europe is home to vultures, four species in fact, and they not only belong to this continent but they are vital to many of the ecosystems found here. In some places, vultures are common, a feature of azure blue skies and the harsh landscapes below them. Extremadura in central western Spain is one of these places. It is a vulture landscape.

I have left the quarry; driven back down the twisting, winding road; crossed the trapped, shackled, still and sedate Tajo via a Roman bridge that defines this part of the region; and then driven up around more bends to the town perched on the hill. A quick passage through a maze of narrow cobbled streets and I find myself atop an arch that once served as a defensive gate high above the only crossing of the Tajo for miles around. It would have been chosen for

The magnificent Roman bridge of Alcántara has spanned the Tajo river for nearly two thousand years.

its panoramic view of the countryside, a place to spot all comers long before they got near, this makes it an ideal place to indulge in one of life's pleasures, vulture gazing.

The birds that left the quarry only a few minutes before are now scattered dots across the sky, some are so far away that it's momentarily possible to get their dots confused with the myriad of hirundines and swifts that are filling the air above the valley, feeding on an invisible updraft of insects. I lie on my back and gaze upwards, my vision detached from the land around me, all I can see is the blue and the birds that thrive within it. Vulture gazing is hypnotic. Follow a Griffon on its smooth glide across the sky and you will get a literal understanding of freedom; your mind can empty itself of all the clutter that we humans accumulate in our consciousness. Relax and watch the bird. The clattering bills of White Storks nesting on the top of the ruined convent next to the arch only add to the soporific feeling induced by this mental tracing of aerial routes. I often wonder what sort of picture they would paint if the blue sky was canvas and their seemingly endless drifting were brush strokes. One thing is certain though, it would be no random Jackson Pollack.

To us, their movement across the sky seems like meanderings with no real purpose, but to think that is to underestimate. If you leave the reverie of vulture gazing for a moment and enter the world of vulture watching, you will notice just how much the bird above you is turning its head and neck, positioning its flight constantly so that it can observe all – observing the terrain beneath it, the behaviour of other species and observing the other vultures it can see in the sky. This is their strategy. They don't just read the air, they read all.

The colony from the quarry is now dispersed across the Extremaduran landscape, most are out of sight for me, and also for the Griffons that are in the air above me, but these birds are still visually connected to one another via a visibility chain. The bird above me can't see its fellow colony member drifting over the plains down towards the Rio Salor valley in the south, after all the bird is dozens of kilometres away from it now, but it can see one bird circling off to the west, and that bird can see one off to the south, and that bird can see one further south again, and, well, you get the picture. The vultures are not randomly placed across the sky; they make sure they are always able to see at least one other bird and, in this way, they are connected to not just the other members of their colony, but also to the many other colonies situated in the area. It's an information network.

Later in the day, I am nearer home, out on the vast wide-open plain that lies on the northern side of the Rio Salor. The plain is alive with bird song, the rich flowing song of larks abound – Crested, Short-toed and, most dominant of all, the large heavy-billed Calandra. Spring is the time of year to be out in this openness. The fields are carpeted in a mixture of yellows, purples and whites, the wild flowers disguising the usually bland covering of green, and lying over this, over the tracks that criss-cross the area, is this smothering blanket of liquid sound. Smothering might imply something oppressive, but not in this context. The bird song is smothering out our sounds. I can't hear humans, their cars or their machines; all I can hear is beauty. The human world smothered into silence by birds.

Calandra Larks are completely tied to this habitat. As soon as the plains start to break up into Cistus scrub they vanish from the skies, they are abundantly everywhere on the grassy steppe-like habitat they call home, but none stray beyond it. They are magnificent songsters, competing against one another to be heard, the overall volume is simply immense. To be out on the Extremaduran plain in the spring, surrounded by wild flowers and smothered by lark song is an experience that should not be missed. I can't get enough of it. This is very much a bird-dominated landscape and its cast of performers is like a must-see list for any European birder, from the tiny Zitting Cisticola to the huge Great Bustard, from the ridiculous rainbow of colour that is the Bee-eater to the militaristically camouflaged Stone Curlew, from the furious flight of a Little Bustard to the floating flight of a Montagu's Harrier – this habitat has it all. It is dramatic birding in an undramatic landscape.

These plains aren't completely flat; they undulate across the landscape. These large open vistas give an impression of flatness and, if you saw a picture of it, it wouldn't look very exciting. However, a photo of this landscape doesn't capture its essence, and in this case the camera does lie. What you would see is a vast grassland landscape dotted with occasional beef cattle and Merino sheep, but you would miss the vibrant birdlife that is throughout.

Some Ravens make their delightful cronking call some distance away from me, and I look over in the direction it came from to notice a Black Kite descending downwards until it is hidden from me by an undulation; the Raven flies slowly above the spot where the kite disappeared. To an untrained eye this might not mean anything, but if you read it with the eye of a vulture it may well mean everything. I get in the car and drive along the track to the next rise. As the cloud of dust that envelops the car when I stop begins to dissipate, I

Ravens are always quick to spot feeding opportunities and the vultures know this.

can see the Black Kite on the ground. To its left is a Raven, and in between them is a dead sheep. It is lying stricken in the middle of a huge closely cropped field, its legs sticking upwards – it looks like it has been dumped here and it probably has. If you want to get rid of a dead sheep, leaving it out in the middle of the plain is a sure way of doing so. Farmers know this, and as I quickly scan about I pick up the telltale trace of dust hanging in the air that indicates a vehicle has only recently driven off. The cronk of the Raven was no doubt in response to this vehicle's arrival in the field – Ravens are clever birds; they learn quickly the significance of what they see.

I read the significance of the Black Kite and the Raven and I know I won't be the only one to have done so. Jumping out of the car I immediately see the first Griffon making a long descent towards the ovine casualty. It is not flapping its wings but, using its aerodynamics to perfection, it is moving rapidly through the sky. This bird saw what I saw and knew what it could mean. The vulture information network will be kicking into action and, sure enough, I can see more from all points of the compass, heading this way and doing so with the seemingly effortless speed of the first. As soon as that first Griffon Vulture changed course to watch what the Black Kite and the Raven were doing, a ripple of interest spread through the vultures spaced out across the sky. Those that could see the first bird would have reacted to its change in behaviour, and that reaction would have been reacted to by the birds that could see those birds, and so on. As soon as the first bird started to lose height, the others would have immediately followed, which, in turn, would have been followed by the next birds in the chain of visibility. The sky is suddenly full of these magnificent birds coming from everywhere. A few minutes ago, I couldn't see one; now I can see dozens and dozens. They have formed a huge circling mass over the plain – hungry they might be, but they are also characteristically cautious and they are checking for danger, waiting for the first bird to descend before they then follow. Two birds lower their long legs down to break their aerodynamic shape and they drop out of the sky to land beside the sheep. As soon as they waddle their way over to the wool-wrapped package of meat, the others forget their reticence and suddenly it's raining vultures.

I start to count the birds as they land, and within a minute I am up to sixty and there are many still descending. Once they land, the patient bide-your-time behaviour of the morning becomes an angry free-for-all of flashing beaks, slapping wings and strange unearthly noises as each bird tries to secure itself a meal. They are not the only vultures to have come – an adult Egyptian Vulture stands slightly aloof from the mass of feeding

When a carcass is detected, the sky above it can fill rapidly with vultures.

A Griffon Vulture descends to join the throng feeding on the plain.

Griffons. It, too, would have read what was happening, but its smaller size won't gain it a place at the table. It will have to wait, but it will feed. Griffons like muscle tissue, but the Egyptian is not so fussy and will happily clear up any trodden, dirt-coated entrails that remain. Another species of vulture arrives, but this one doesn't wait on the sidelines – it lands and barges its way through to the carcass whilst the Griffons part reluctantly to allow it space. Size matters, and when it comes to size even the mighty Griffon Vulture loses out to the Black Vulture.

I have been told that five minutes after the first Griffon Vulture lands at a sheep carcass there is nothing left. Well, today I made it about seven minutes. Suddenly the vigorous hustle reduces, the birds that are still gathering in the sky continue to circle rather than drop down and many of those on the ground have waddled away a few metres. There are one hundred and three Griffon Vultures, three Black Vultures and two Egyptian Vultures on the ground. There are another twenty Griffons immediately above and further out there are more, but they are reading the situation from afar and know they are too late. Of the carcass, only the major bones remain. Wildlife's environmental cleaners have done their job. The Egyptian Vultures and Black Kites are poised to clear up any remnants. Come tomorrow, the only sign of what happened here will be a few scattered white bones.

With their crops noticeably bulging, the Griffon Vultures stand quietly by, the cordiality between individuals has been restored and they stand together, quite literally letting their food go down. The three Black Vultures are dispersed amongst the Griffons, their dark plumage and size giving them an almost authoritarian look. With a wingspan of around three metres, the Black Vulture is a huge bird. The three I can see have probably come from the visible Sierra de San Pedro, a range of hills that flanks the southern side of the Rio Salor valley as these plains flank the north. This small range of hills has the highest density of breeding Black Vultures anywhere in the world, with just under four hundred pairs. Unlike the Griffons, they are tree nesters and their massive nests both defy the limits of gravity and your imagination in equal measure.

The bubbly calls of Black-bellied Sandgrouse tear me away from watching the vultures and, swinging around to my right, I find a small flock of five birds flying low and fast over the plain, behind them are three stragglers. Their frantic flight is a million miles away from that of the vultures. They flash their black bellies as they fly, making them conspicuous in the bright landscape, before dropping down into a ploughed field and becoming far harder to see. They can be notoriously hard to spot, but over the years I have got to know where they are likely to be and I do often see them, but by far the best way of finding them is to learn their flight call. Both they, and their cousin, the Pin-tailed Sandgrouse, have distinctive calls and in this three-hundred-and-sixty-degree landscape it is these calls that alert you to their presence, for you never seem to be looking in the direction they are flying from. I can hear the raspberry of a Little Bustard drifting on the wind, but it is faint and very hard to pinpoint the direction it is coming from. Another plains dweller with a distinctive call, the Little Bustard has declined worryingly in recent years and although it is relatively easy to find on these plains, the locals tell me the sad tale, often heard, of how much rarer they are nowadays. Their call is a sound that carries a long way and you can be convinced that it is much nearer to you than it actually is. This one is so faint that it could be many hundreds of metres away from me, and I have little chance of spotting it, especially as I can't even locate in which direction to search. I return to the vultures.

Those on the ground are all loafing now, digesting their bolted-down meal with their powerful digestive juices dissolving all. The immediate sky above is beginning to empty of them, some drift in and have a look at their sated friends, but without any food left to hold their interest they drift onwards, spreading themselves out over the landscape again, re-establishing those visibility chains once more. It is another great opportunity to partake in some vulture gazing and I readily do so.

In the evening, I head off on my habitual walk around the village's small reservoir. The sun above me is heading westwards and the vultures are heading back to their roosting sites either to the south in the sierra or to the north in the gorge like Salor valley. Their silhouettes are distinctive against the reddening sky – the Black Vulture has a plank-like rectangular shape to its wings with the trailing edge, parallel with the front, looking at times like the teeth of a saw; the Griffon's, by contrast, has a more bulging shape to the trailing edge of the wing, giving it a more smoothed curved appearance. The Black flies on flat, level wings; the Griffon on wings held in a shallow V-shape. There are several of each in the sky and some of the Griffons heading to the sierra will no doubt be birds from earlier today – they have probably spent the rest of their day out on the plain, slowly digesting their food and are only now heading back to their roosting and breeding sites. Tomorrow it starts again, but not too early.

MAY

Of the four vulture species that are breeding in southern Europe, three of them – the Griffon, the Black and the Egyptian – are common in Extremadura, but the fourth is only a very rare visitor, although it is an increasing one. The Bearded Vulture is on the comeback trail thanks largely to direct conservation methods and a very successful captive breeding and reintroduction project that should be an inspiration to all conservationists. Many know this giant vulture by its Germanic name of Lammergeier, but this name is being largely dropped nowadays to distance these massive, majestic scavengers from the fabricated origin of that label. Bearded Vultures don't kill lambs, but we humans are not always the most enlightened, nor are we always rational and the Bearded Vulture was wiped out from the vast majority of its European range because we mistakenly thought it a threat to our livestock.

These huge vultures were still breeding in Extremadura at the beginning of the twentieth century, but soon disappeared from here and most of the Iberian Peninsula, with only a very small number hanging on in the remote rugged Pyrenees. Things are very different a century later – there are now over two hundred and fifty mature individuals in the Pyrenees and there has been some natural spread to the mountains immediately to the west of this impressive range, which forms the border between France and Spain. However, the big change has come about thanks to the conservation work and reintroduction projects that have now led to a breeding population re-establishing itself in the Sierra de Cazorla in southern Spain where over fifty birds have been reared and released as part of the project. The birds are released as youngsters in a process known as hacking and, as young vultures do, they wander huge distances, returning to the release area when they are ready to breed several years later. Many of these birds wander north and into Extremadura, where they have been seen during all the months of the year in various mountain ranges within the region. However, the main area of sightings is the mighty Sierra de Gredos that runs like a central spine across Spain, extending into the very north-eastern part of Extremadura.

Some of these wandering birds have stayed in the region for extended periods, with one bird present in the Gredos range for eighteen continuous months. The Bearded Vulture doesn't breed until it is at least five years old and, so far, these long-staying birds have not remained in the area once they have reached maturity, returning instead to the Sierra de Cazorla, their release site. It is here that they are now breeding again, starting the recolonisation process with their own wild-born young. Will these bone-eating specialists return to being an Extremaduran breeding bird again? It will take time, but as the population of these birds continues to slowly increase, as the breeding population in the south develops and as the conservation effort continues, surely the Bearded Vulture will return to join the Griffon, the Black and the Egyptian in this vulture landscape.

A young Griffon Vulture chick, sitting in the small collection of untidy sticks that make up its rudimentary nest perched high up on a rocky ledge, looks out on the world from under the shadow of its parent, which is strategically placed to keep the sun off the growing chick. Around it, Crag Martins buzz the sky, performing acrobatic manoeuvres as they pluck tiny insects out of the air. Above them, and above the snaggle-tooth rocky ridge, Alpine Swifts slice their way through the blue with their razor-sharp wings, their art deco streamline shape emphasised by their equally deco black and white livery. These large swifts quite literally live in the air, staying airborne for more than two hundred days at a time. They have no use for the ground other than for breeding and, when they do breed, they select steep cliff faces with fissures. Even when they do touch the ground, the ground they touch is vertical.

The adult vulture ignores these smaller birds, but the chick, developing fast on its less than appetising diet of regurgitated carrion, watches them with vague interest. It has to spend many more long days just watching from the ledge it is on before it can attempt its first, inevitably clumsy, flight. Watching vulture nests is not an exciting affair, nothing much happens. The chick will occasionally break the monotony by snapping its beak at a bothersome fly, but that's about it. The real excitement in watching vulture nests comes in the places you have to be in to do so. They are wild places, places where our species is not comfortable or numerous. Places like this – a rocky arc of hills on the western edge of the

In the spring, lavender forms purple carpets across many areas.

region with Portugal visible on the horizon. All three of Extremadura's vulture species are breeding around me: the small colony of Griffons loosely scattered across the rocky ledges; a pair of Egyptians sequestered away in a small cave on a spur of rock that drops down to the now almost dry stream; and, in a large pine behind the cliff face from where I am watching the young Griffon, an even younger Black Vulture chick sits patiently in its tree nest. Humans may not be comfortable in this landscape, but like the vultures they are here and they have been here on many occasions. Overhead the clear blue sky is lined with the evaporating white snail trails of our planes, and the purple of the lavender and the brilliant white of the Cistus flowers reverberate with bees busy collecting their wares to take back to the row of hives tucked away under some nearby Evergreen Oaks. Where this ridge descends and breaks to allow a stream to pass through it, is where the most profound sign of humans in the landscape can be found. Hidden, in what is now an almost inaccessible cave, are the painted hand outlines of past human residents from five thousand years ago.

When I am here, and I am here often as it is one of my favourite places, I wonder how this area would have looked to those who once occupied the cave compared to how it looks now. I can't imagine it would have looked hugely different. It would certainly be recognisable to me, the hard physical geography of the area won't have changed much in those five millennia, save for the odd rock displacing itself and tumbling to the floor. The small patch of cultivated Olive trees wouldn't be there, nor would the string of introduced eucalypts delineating the course of the stream, but other than that, the Cistus scrub would probably still dominate much as it does now. And the Vultures would be here.

But not all the birds present now would have been here five thousand years ago; some wouldn't have even been here fifty years ago. The cave, which once provided shelter for people, now provides a nest site for one of Europe's most recent avian colonists, the White-rumped Swift. This African swift has slowly, but surely, been colonising southern Spain since the mid-1960s as it expands its range northwards and there are now a number of sites scattered across Extremadura. I discovered the birds here in 2012 and they have been here every year since then. Like the other three species of swift present (the Alpine, Pallid and Common) the White-rumped Swifts are migrants, but unlike the other three, these are late arrivals, arriving now in May.

There are plenty of small, potentially swift-shaped birds dashing around the rock faces and the sky-filled gap in the ridge above the cave, but these are mainly Crag Martins and House Martins, whose flash of white on the rump is enormously eye-catching when looking for the unrelated, but also white-rumped, swift. Red-rumped Swallows are also present and their pale rump can trick the eye momentarily before you register their much more dainty flight. They have to be here because no red rumps mean no white rumps.

The White-rumped Swift is, in our humanised view of the world, a bit of a bully. They arrive late to breed, but they can afford to do so because the laborious task of building a nest is not for them – they are not builders, they are dispossessors. They take over a freshly built Red-rumped Swallow's nest, actively forcing the smaller swallows out, either aggressively chasing them off or simply flying into the unguarded nest and refusing to leave it. Red-rumped Swallow nests are a work of art, a painstaking, laborious one. Using tiny beak-fills of mud they build their structure on the underside of rocky overhangs, inside caves, etc. Their nest consists of a dome-shaped cup with a long tunnel entrance and it can take the small hirundines up to two weeks to build. They are beautifully architectural in their construction, an avian work of art and the White-rumped Swift obviously approves of their design, for it is always these nests that it usurps for its own.

As I watch for these colonising nest thieves, I can hear the beautiful fluty call of a Golden Oriole floating up from the tall Eucalyptus away to my right, as well as the raucous, rasping calls of a group of Azure-winged Magpies foraging through the patchy scrub that clothes the gentle slope down to the stream bed. I try not to let them distract me as I scan for the White-rumped Dasher that I am looking for, but then another call echoes off the rock and this one does distract me. It is the harsh, barking call of a spectacular bird, a bird that is another reason why I spend so much time at this site – the truly imperious Spanish Imperial Eagle.

There is something exciting about eagles, something that gets inside you. There are five species in this vulture landscape. The spring and summer-visiting Booted and Short-toed are great birds to behold, but it is the resident trio that really gets you. There's the Bonelli's, the Golden and the Imperial – all three are majestic, all three give you a kick of endorphins when you see them, but for me it has to be the Imperial. These iconic endemics almost crashed out of existence a few decades ago, struggling to survive in the modern, human-dominated world, but they have bounced back and numbers have steadily increased. A fine piece of conservation effort has seen that these birds are now able to fill up the available territories in this part of Extremadura. The Imperials reign once again.

The white leading edges of the dark, almost black, wings flash in the ever-present sunlight as the bird powers its way past the rocky ridge and into my view. It is the resident male and he is slightly smaller than the female with less white blazed across his shoulders, but he is still impressive to behold. He barks again, demanding my attention, before banking sharply on his flat, dark wings to enter a spiralling flow of air to lift him up and away. He gains height with speed and ease, and he soon becomes a small silhouette in the bright sky. I feel the buzz of seeing him, the awe. I see him a lot, but that buzz never diminishes. Spanish Imperial Eagles are awesome birds in the truest sense of the word. An apex predator buzz – you just can't beat it.

With the eagle high, I turn my head back down again to where a male Subalpine Warbler watches me curiously from within the waxy-leafed confines of a Cistus bush before scolding me for my impertinence in being there and dashing off into thicker cover to continue his noisy, harsh chastisement. Suitably admonished, I return my focus to the gap of the ridge. There are three or four Alpine Swift chasing about and then I get a brief glimpse of a smaller swift shape that vanishes behind the foreground of rock. I wait, expectantly, hoping that it will reappear. Numerous Crag and House Martins scud across my binoculars, but no small swift. I shift my gaze leftwards following the irregular, broken skyline of the rocky ridge, and there it is, finally. A White-rumped Swift gliding through the air, the sickle shape and deeply forked tail so distinctive I wonder how it was possible to get momentarily confused with the hirundines. The light highlights the white rump and even the small white edge on the secondaries as the bird turns towards me and then twists away again, giving me a prolonged view as it feeds over the uneven skyline of rock. When these birds first turned up in the sixties, people didn't think that they could be White-rumped Swifts because they were expecting another, more predictable coloniser, the Little Swift. But that's the beauty about nature – it is always full of surprises.

I lower the binoculars and look about me, taking in the area, the thick impenetrable scrub, the multiple lines of irregular rocky ridges and the serried ranks of the Olives. One of the Egyptian Vultures is in the air, its white wedge-shaped tail translucent against the bright sky; a small stack of Griffon Vultures is gradually drifting this way and, a long way off, a Short-toed Eagle is hovering against a background of the hills of eastern Portugal, eyes fixed downwards, scrutinising the ground below it. This snake hunter is hunting, hanging in the wind on its long wings, head held stock-still intently focused on the ground below.

The Griffons are a lot closer now, they are returning to the ridge and have gradually lost height from when I first saw them. As they pass over me I can hear their wings shearing through the air, making a sound like a distant jet, an exhilarating rush of noise. Reading the air and understanding its routes, they circle off to the right, before the first one banks sharply, folds its large wings slightly back and lowers its long legs and large feet to both break up the aerodynamics of the streamlined body and to also apply the air brakes. Landing on a narrow shelf of rock takes precision, if they come in too fast, they risk smacking hard in to the unyielding rock; too slow and they will stall too early. This one, as they always seem to do, judges it to perfection, the wings fold back a bit more and the bird drops downwards at an angle towards the towering wall of rock. About ten metres away from it, the bird opens its wings out again, tilts them back and gets just enough lift to raise up and reach the ledge at the same time that its forward momentum peters out. It steps out of the air and on to the rock, as easily as you or I would step out of a lift and on to the landing.

Vulture gazing can lead your mind off on many paths and, as I gaze at the other birds carrying out identical landings, my mind wanders and wonders. Watching a vulture coming in to land on a ledge is so common place that you can get a bit blasé about it, but

A Griffon Vulture applying the air brakes by lowering its legs and breaking up the aerodynamic air flow as it comes in to land.

that large bird with a wingspan not far short of three metres has just dropped out of the sky and landed on a ledge maybe half a metre deep surrounded by large unforgiving walls of solid rock. What calculations does the bird's brain need to carry out to judge the angle and speed of descent, to spot the exact moment it needs to lift up again and stall its flight? This must be complicated enough without having to factor in the wind speed, its direction and how the sun or cloud is affecting the way the air is moving around the multifaceted rock face. It can't just be instinctive. Sometimes you will see a bird come in and abort its attempt, pulling out of their descent and banking away from the cliff before gaining height to try again. To realise that the conditions aren't right, or that the angle or speed of descent is wrong, demonstrates a level of thought process.

Near Santander in northern Spain, a colony of Griffon Vultures have taken this ledge nesting to the extreme, building their nests on ledges on a huge coastal headland of towering rocky sea cliffs. Just under a hundred pairs breed above the waves, the only coastal nesting vultures in Europe, and they share the ledges with gulls and shags rather than swifts and Blue Rock Thrushes. These nesting vultures have to factor in the strong air currents driven by the Bay of Biscay's stormy reputation when they come in to land. But, like their land-locked relations, they do so with their typical ease.

Musing on thoughts of vultures battling coastal gales, I start to slowly head back along the track. A Woodlark catches my eye as it lands on a long-fallen piece of wood that is gradually crumbling, slowly being recycled back to the soil from whence it originally came. The short tail and the wonderful white supercilium eye stripe readily distinguish it from the many other small brown birds present. The small bill of this delightful singer is crammed full of insects, revealing to me that it has a nest with young nearby. It doesn't move a muscle as it watches me warily – it won't go in to feed whilst I am there. The nests of these ground dwellers, and the chicks within, are flawlessly camouflaged in the vegetation somewhere on the ground close by, but the bird won't give it away. It will eat the food itself and fly off to get more, rather than run in to its nest whilst I am present. I smile at the perfectly motionless bird and leave it to relax as I continue down the stony track, heading onwards, past the Olives and their silvery green leaves that are fluttering in a slight breeze.

Crossing the line of puddles, which won't flow as a stream again for several more months, I spot a male Sardinian Warbler having a vigorous bath, a blur of wings and water spray with a black cap. This normally vigilant bird seems totally oblivious to my presence as he washes the dust out of his feathers. He plunges in and out of the puddle three or four times, immersing totally, before a final energetic shake down followed by a short flight to a patch of rampant brambles where he sits on a straggly thorn-laden branch that has poked its way out of the marauding green mass. He has deliberately chosen this exposed perch because it won't take him long to dry off in the sun.

From deep within the brambles, a song of pure liquidity bursts forth, drenching me in its beauty. Somewhere inside the thorn-fortified fortress of green a Nightingale sings its serenade, loud, clear and pure, the notes tumble in perfection. All other sound seems to stop. The bramble is impenetrable to my eye, but not to my ear and I listen and enjoy the unseen maestro of bird song for several minutes before it suddenly and abruptly stops. A small, brown rusty-tinged bird slopes off from the back of the bramble clump, flying up the route of the watercourse and disappearing into another mass of thick vegetation. The liquid song starts again from this new location, further off but still glorious. Nightingales are nothing to look at, but they are everything to hear. An audible delight.

Further up the track, where the scrub starts to give way to trees, a Woodchat Shrike drops out of the bottom of a small, neatly rounded Evergreen Oak. The flame-red of its head flares in the sunlight contrasting with the black and white of its wings and body, it snaffles something in the grass before flying back up to its perch in the tree – a short, dead branch hanging down out of the densely leafed canopy, the perfect spot to spend the afternoon completely enveloped in the cool shade and with an all-round view of the ground beneath it.

A beautiful gem of a Bee-eater zips across the track in front of me, flashing colour as it snatches something out of the air and then drops and glides to the fence line. The little flying rainbow lands on the wire next to one of the metal posts, its saturated colours standing out boldly against the monochromatic vegetation behind. With an unexpected violence, it suddenly smears the rear end of the insect held tightly in its bill against the rusted metal of the post, first one way and then the other. Satisfied that the literal sting in the tail is no more, it sits up and swallows its catch whole. Something catches the bird's eye and it skews its head upwards, watching intently, and then it is in motion again, a blur of colour shooting vertically up to catch its next mouthful. Down it glides again to the fence and this time it sits still and I can see that the insect held tightly in the black tweezer-like

The Bee-eater is, perhaps, Europe's most exotic-looking bird, a real living rainbow.

bill is a pretty blue butterfly. There is no smearing this time, no painful sting to dislodge, a jewel of the insect world to feed a jewel of the bird world.

The butterfly-eating Bee-eater is joined on the fence by another, most probably its mate. They sit there together for a few moments refracting their exotic, tropical-looking colours in the sunlight and then they are away, triangular wings busy as they dash over the countryside in pursuit of their insect quarry. They are simply stunning birds, an exotic palette, an almost unbelievable mix of reds, yellows and blues, finished off with a few delicate black touches.

The sky is empty now, other than a solitary Egyptian Vulture, with its immaculate white and black plumage of its underside contrasting brilliantly against the background of blue sky. The third member of the Extremaduran vulture club is a lot smaller than the gargantuan Black and Griffon and, because of this, it is easy to forget that it is actually a big bird in its own right, with a wingspan similar to that of a Grey Heron. The Egyptian can often be seen around farm buildings, especially where there is a concentration of livestock. They are somewhat catholic in their dietary requirements – they don't specialise in the carcasses of large mammals like the Griffon does; indeed, their weaker, smaller bill isn't strong enough to tear muscle and tissue like its bigger relatives. These smaller vultures will eat all sorts of organic matter as well as carrion, and will often feed on animal waste and afterbirth and the insects that these attract. The local Spanish dialect knows them as 'churretero', dung eater. It's not wrong. Near towns and villages, they can often be found stalking the local rubbish tip, gleaning out meals from our own wasteful habits or visiting the sewage farms. At a large mammal carcass, they are normally forced to wait on the side lines whilst the bigger and more dominant Blacks and Griffons feed voraciously. Occasionally, an Egyptian will be able to sneak in and grab something, but usually they bide their time, going in after the others have gorged themselves to clean the last ragged remnants of flesh off the bones and to hoover up any viscera left in the dirt. When it comes to environmental clean-ups, Egyptian Vultures do the dirtiest work.

Egyptians have a very distinctive silhouette in flight, with their wedge-shaped tail and broad rectangular wings offset by a small head and tiny bill. Closer views reveal that they are strange-looking birds, with their triangular-shaped wrinkly yolk-yellow face surrounded by a shock of white feathers that stick up in an unruly hairstyle manner around the back of the head, making them look, in my probably twisted imagination, a bit like Doc Brown from Back to the Future.

These arc birds that could do with a time machine to take them back to a time when their numbers weren't as low as they are now. Watching this vulture serenely gliding through the air, it is easy to forget just how much their European population has fallen in recent years. Spain is their European stronghold, with an estimated one thousand pairs, but even here the numbers have fallen in the last few decades. But it is elsewhere in southern Europe where the fall has been most worrying. France was once another bastion for the Egyptian, but the population there suffered a strong decline, although thankfully this has now stabilised at around eighty-five pairs. Italy and the Balkans have also seen catastrophic losses, and the Italian population is now in danger of disappearing altogether.

The causes for these declines are many and are muddied by the fact that the Egyptian Vulture is a migratory species, mainly spending the winter months away from Europe in sub-Saharan Africa. However, it is clear in Europe that the principle causes of mortality are, unsurprisingly, all down to us. Electrocution via collisions with power lines has long been an issue for this (and many other) species. In more recent years collisions with wind turbines have also become a real problem, particularly when those turbines are situated on migration routes. But perhaps the biggest cause of adult mortality in Europe is poisoning.

The Egyptian Vulture is not deliberately targeted; it is an innocent unwitting victim of an illegal activity, but due to its feeding habits, it is vulnerable to both direct and indirect poisoning. Vultures often occur in areas where mammalian predators are also

With its spiky crown and wrinkled yellow face, the Egyptian Vulture is an unusual looking bird.

found. In Europe these predators include the wolf and the fox, both of which are regularly, and illegally, targeted by poisoners. In the past, large animal carcasses were placed out, deliberately laced with toxins to kill wolves and foxes that fed on them. This inevitably killed birds as well, with everything from Griffon Vultures through to Robins being found dead alongside these lethal baits. Thanks to increased awareness and enforcement of legislation, the days of a landowner leaving a poisoned sheep or cow carcass out in full view have gone. Unfortunately, the urge to poison our wildlife hasn't. To conceal their illegal activities, the modern-day wildlife poisoner leaves small pieces of lethally laced meat under the cover of bushes and shrubs. These aren't noticeable to people and are hard for the enforcement agencies to detect, but they are easily found by foxes and other mammals. Sadly, the Egyptian Vulture, which spends large amounts of time foraging on the ground, also finds them.

Egyptian Vultures, unlike their bigger European cousins, are quite happy to scavenge carcasses of small animals and birds and this can make them vulnerable to the ingestion of lead shot. A pigeon shot as it flew overhead may fall beyond the reach of the hunter, but it won't be beyond the reach of the scavenger. Lead poisoning of Egyptian Vultures is now a serious concern for conservationists and is a significant factor in their mortality in many places throughout their range.

The increase in adult mortality has unfortunately led indirectly to an increase in mortality in first-year birds as they embark on their first migration back across the Mediterranean Sea to Africa. Although the Spanish birds have a relatively short crossing at the Straits of Gibraltar, the Italian and Balkan birds have a far longer one and it is on this crossing that these young birds are frequently running into trouble. In the past, with larger numbers of adults around, young birds would follow the more experienced birds across the open sea; now, due to the dwindling numbers of adults, the young birds are attempting the crossing alone. Their inexperience can lead them into making mistakes in direction, meaning that they fly for far longer than they need to, causing the birds to become exhausted and, for some, their migration attempt ends in the waters of the Med. This is the stereotypical vicious circle: lower numbers of adults lead to higher mortality in young; higher mortality in young leads to lower numbers of adults. The vicious circle is also an ever-decreasing one. The numbers are stark. In the last forty years, Europe has lost fifty per cent of its Egyptian Vultures, and now only about one in seven of the young hatched survive to be breeding adults themselves.

There is hope. Various conservation projects are now underway in various countries, including one in the Douro gorge on the Spain/Portugal border a few hundred kilometres north of where I am standing. The work throughout Europe involves lobbying parliaments and regional assemblies, educating and informing the wider public and liaising with the electric supply companies to modify pylons to reduce the very real risk of electrocution. This latter work has been backed up recently in the courts in Spain where electric companies have been heavily fined for failing to carry out safeguarding works, setting an expensive precedent for those that do not do so in the future. Sadly, trying to change the small-minded mentality of the poisoners is very difficult. Instead, effort has focused on educating the law enforcement agencies, and funding and training has been provided to establish anti-poisoning teams comprised of specially trained dogs and handlers that will hopefully be able to locate the poisoned bait before the vultures and other wildlife find it. Wildlife poisoning is a heinously selfish crime that has the potential to have devastating knock-on effects in the local environment.

Watching the bird above me carefully searching the land below it for a meal, it seems a world away from the troubles we cause, but the harsh reality is, *that* world – *our* world – is also this bird's. Unaware of my profound thoughts concerning it, the bird continues to drift over the landscape of scrub, trees and Olive groves, scrutinising everything below it for a feeding opportunity. There will be potentially two young chicks, sitting in the scruffy collection of twigs that make up their nest in the small cave in the cliff, waiting hungrily for the result of its flight.

JUNE

Sitting on a thick bed of long, soft, slender pine needles that have gathered over the years below the large gnarled and twisted tree that is providing me with much-needed shade, I look again into the viewfinder of my telescope. The huge chick, a gangly mix of black feathers and dark wispy down, is sitting in the huge nest that has quite literally flattened the top of the tree. It is still in the same hunched-over position, its bill open as it pants to regulate its body temperature in the relentless sunshine. Black Vulture nests are ridiculous. They are huge gargantuan structures for huge gargantuan birds.

A breeding pair will reuse the previous year's nest, adding more material, stick after stick, year after year, increasing the structure in bulk and size. They get enormous and can be two metres across and up to three metres in depth. They are amongst the biggest bird nests in the world and, considering the diet of the birds, they must be a whole ecosystem in themselves, an entomological paradise waiting to be discovered. The trees chosen for these nests become deformed, twisted, misshapen relics of what they once were, buckled by the sheer bulk of the nest. From the time the chick first chisels its way out of the egg to the time when it steps off the nest into the unknown world of flight takes just under four months.

A Black Vulture in flight, gargantuan birds with an almost three-metre wingspan.

This bird has another five, maybe six weeks of seemingly endless waiting in the nest. June is hot in this vulture landscape, but July and August are even hotter and there is no escape from the sun in a tree-top nest – the young vulture has no choice but to simply endure.

I am surrounded by rolling ridges, clothed in dense greens of thick vegetation interrupted only where the rocks rip through this scrubby fabric, jutting upwards in randomly angular formations. The heady scent of the Cistus scrub, so potent in the sunshine, blends with the clean fresh aroma of the pines. I am breathing in the landscape as well as seeing it. Bird song abounds from all around me, fluty Woodlarks, scratchy warblers and the evocative two-note signature of spring – the cuckoo – all ringing in my ears. It is a landscape for the senses.

Around me, in the Pine-spotted Cistus scrub, various Sylvia warblers are busy. I have already seen the constantly active Sardinian and Dartford (two English names that are delightfully incongruous here) bouncing their way through the twiggy labyrinth of the Cistus branches, occasionally breaking through the top to sing, before once again entering the multi-layered world below. Now, a few metres away, a beautiful Subalpine male, hopping about in all its plumatic glory of reds and greys offset with a thin, bandit-like white moustache, is engrossed in gathering food from the base of a straggly, seedling pine. A Thekla Lark, more subdued, more practical in its colouration, meanders its way in little dashes through the shady scrub, pausing to look at me for a second or two, cocking its head as it does so, unsure of what my seated form represents. It dismisses me; I am no more than a momentary curiosity for it and on it dashes through the scrub. In the pine above me, I hear the happy, tumbling trill of a Crested Tit and soon spot it as it hangs acrobatically on sewing needle-thin legs to probe the underside of the branches, gleaning aphids and small caterpillars from them. All around me is alive with birds, but the sky is empty, the morning has moved on and the raptorial riches of this region are evidently enjoying some down time. I have one more last look at the still panting chick, mentally wish it well and then make my move, provoking a wave of Sylvia scolding from all around.

As I pick up the fire break-cum-track, I spook a group of Red Deer, young males, sleek and agile, their velvet-covered antlers softening their appearance as they move briskly away from me, their hooves clicking away on the stony surface. They don't go far before their innate curiosity causes them to stop and turn back to eye my movements suspiciously. They are stock-still except for the slow chewing of jaws and the occasional fly-dislodging twitch of the ears. This group of six males will soon start to fray off that velvet covering, revealing the hard bone beneath, ready for the forthcoming September rut when a testosterone grenade will explode their tight little group. Standing in the shade of some Cork Oaks as they watch me, it is obvious that they see me as a novelty rather than as a threat. They should be more wary though – it is not just the rut that arrives with a bang in September, the shooting season does too.

The part of the Sierra de San Pedro that lies on the south side of the main road to neighbouring Portugal is a wonderfully wild place, but it is hard to access, much harder than the other parts of this vulture landscape. There are few public roads that cross it and the tracks that run from them are invariably gated and signed with lightly veiled threats of security guards and response teams. This is the area of the large shooting estate, the rich man's playground. Princes, Sheikhs and various ranks of nobility from all over the world own the land in this small slither of Extremadura and they don't want to share it.

In many places, Britain especially, huge shooting estates can inevitably mean deliberate and sustained persecution of raptors, black holes into which these birds disappear, but that is not the case here. There are no Pheasants, no Red Grouse to blast, the hunter's quarry is mammalian and the Red Deer is very much top of the list. Closing off the land here is a controversial topic, but the one thing it does do is provide a large area of relatively undisturbed terrain within which the raptor population thrives. These shut-off hills

Winding its way through the Sierra de San Pedro, this track
is flanked by flowering Broom and Cistus in the spring.

provide the best area for Black Vulture, Spanish Imperial Eagle and Bonelli's Eagle in the
whole of Extremadura, far better than the famous Monfragüe and its many thousands of
visitors away to the north and east. This land is not shut off for the benefit of raptors; it is
shut off for the few, but those few are at least indifferent to the presence of raptors – they
don't perceive them as a threat to their interests and they don't feel that they need to be
euphemistically managed. I find this area of the Sierra a frustrating, unwelcoming and
uncomfortable place. The only compensation is that the raptors don't.

Immersed in the steep, deep rock-strewn valley of the Rio Salor just to the north of my
village, I watch a newly fledged Griffon Vulture explore its flight potential on the air currents
generated by the rugged geography around us. It turns to circle, instinctively adjusting its
flight feathers as it does so, minute movements to alter the flow of air over the wings. At times
it looks as if it has been flying for years, a veteran of the skies, but then it misjudges its speed
and must flap ungainly, clumsily and energetically to regain control again. Opting for a pause
in its learning curve, it lowers its legs and loses height, coming in to land on a vertical rocky
outcrop on the opposite side of the valley. It is a bumpy landing, but not too bad for a rookie.
It looks at me momentarily, then turns away, looks around and discovers more Griffons
flying, higher up above the valley. It focuses its attention on these, seemingly studying their

movements across the sky. I am of no interest to it, its fellow Griffons are far more interesting than I am, but it does give me a good opportunity to look at the bird more closely.

Newly out of the nest, young Griffons closely resemble the adult birds, but if you look carefully at them, you can see just how neat and even their feathers are, how crisp and pointed the huge finger-like primaries are. Their new plumage has no wear, they haven't undergone any moult, they look pristine, fresh out of the box – because they are. Their body colouration is generally a bit darker than the lighter, more faded full adult plumage, their beaks are still a uniform dark grey and their ruff of feathers is the same brown as their bodies. It is only when they reach full adulthood that their bills become a pale colour and their ruffs become white. Looking at this one through my binoculars I can clearly see how bright and clean the small mini downy feathers that coat the neck and head are. This is a bird that hasn't stuck its head and neck into a carcass yet.

The pure white down on the head and neck, combined with the uniform grey bill and brown ruff, show that this bird is newly fledged from its cliff-ledge nest.

Unlike the bigger Black Vulture, Griffon youngsters fledge in June. The egg in which it developed was laid in late January; those of the Black are laid in late February and early March. Whilst that Black Vulture chick in the Sierra de San Pedro swelters in the sun, trapped in its nest, this young Griffon can fly with freedom through the cooling air currents. It is still dependent on its parents, and it will be for some time to come, but it must be a relief to be able to escape the narrow confines of the nest ledge.

From deep within the young thicket of Narrow-leaved Ash growing below me, an unseen Nightingale pours forth its song, whilst further upstream the soft purring of a Turtle Dove floats down the air currents towards me. Two delights of avian sound, very different from one another, fill the air about me and bring a broad smile to my face. The young vulture on the rock above is oblivious to the sounds below – all its focus is on the circling birds high up. It begins to get fidgety, restless in its repose, this new-found freedom of the skies becoming more and more irresistible.

The young Griffon bundles itself back into the sky, leaving the hard surety of stone for the fluidity of the moving air, the initial heavy wing beats resound across the valley and reflect the effort that went into them. It is not the smooth take-off of an adult, the accomplished step off takes some practice, but it is functional and once it has unfolded those large wings and caught the air beneath them, the youngster rapidly gains height, circling on the updraft, mastering the currents with minimal effort, getting higher with each turn before it disappears over the valley side above me. The sky is busy with vultures, there are lots of Griffon Vultures drifting across it, many of these are convening on an invisible spot where a thermal is evidently providing quick and easy assistance to those that want to be higher, an elevator in the sky. A lone Black Vulture, high up, drifts in the opposite direction and an adult Egyptian Vulture is tightly circling low down, close to one of the pools of water that form the remnants of this river in the early summer. I am watching all three of the Extremaduran vultures in one valley.

But there is potential for another, and I am not talking about the Bearded Vulture. I am talking about a species that was first reported in Spain in 1992, seen at the western edge of the Sierra de San Pedro in Extremadura, just a short Vulture drift from where I am now, in an area where unconfirmed reports of the presence of this species had been coming in since 1990. Rüppell's Vulture, a close relative of the Griffon, is a species found normally in tropical Africa and, like so many of the African species, it is in serious trouble, with the International Union for the Conservation of Nature (IUCN) placing it in the unwanted category of 'Critically Endangered'. There is only one category after Critically Endangered and that is Extinct. This species could be gone forever in just a few years. Considering its extremely perilous position, and the fact that the nearest breeding population is in Senegal in West Africa, it has been a bit of a surprise that this bird has become a somewhat regular visitor to Spain in the last three decades. Every year since that first confirmed sighting, there have been small numbers of these vultures visiting Iberia and, although most of these sightings are in Andalucía in the south where they are beginning to show signs of taking up residence, they have also become rare, but regular, visitors to the vulture landscape of Extremadura.

Rüppell's are slightly smaller than Griffons, darker in plumage than their close cousins, and in a busy vulture-laden sky or in the chaos of a feeding scrum at a carcass they could easily be overlooked. The birds involved in this strange pattern of visits are nearly always immature ones and they are always isolated individuals. Although they are recorded annually in Extremadura, there are probably only one or two individual birds in the region each year – this is no great influx from the south, no invasion, but it is nonetheless very interesting. June is the month in which most sightings occur in Extremadura, but it is certainly a case of being in the right place at the right time if you want to see one.

The young Griffon Vulture that I have just been watching testing out the newly acquired skill of flying won't start to breed until it is four or five years old. Once it is independent of its parents in a couple of months, it will wander widely, potentially covering huge distances. It is probable, but by no means certain, that come the autumn it will join up with other immature birds and cross the narrow band of sea at Gibraltar and head into the continent of Africa where it could remain until well into the next year. Many juvenile and immature Griffon Vultures make this journey and it is likely that, as they make their way back up towards Europe in the spring of the following year, they will encounter and pick up individual young Rüppell's who are themselves also wandering and exploring. These then follow the Griffons back northwards, with some joining them on the crossing into Europe. Once on the European continent the Rüppell's continue to follow the Griffons, hanging around the large breeding colonies of the south and following others up into Extremadura. These young birds are the hitchhikers of the vulture world, joining other youngsters on their nomadic wanderings and popping over to Europe for a bit to see the sights. There have been tales of possible breeding attempts, but it is generally not expected that these birds will stay to breed, there are too few of them. No, these wanderers do their wandering and then they return to an ever increasingly uncertain future.

Populations of African vultures are in freefall. Most, like the Rüppell's, are Critically Endangered and one step away from being a tragic footnote in history. Poisoning is the main reason behind the startling crash in African vultures; they are targeted directly and indirectly and because of their habits they make easy targets. Sentinel poisoning is one of the biggest threats and can virtually wipe out an entire colony in one fell swoop. It is driven by greed, our greed. Poachers kill African mammals to supply the illegal market with animal parts, with ivory and rhino horn being the two main targets. The anti-poaching agencies of Africa have rightly stepped up their game in recent decades to combat this illegal and immoral activity, capturing many poachers in the act. One of the ways of capturing them literally red-handed is to watch what the vultures in the area are doing.

Vultures are the best there is when it comes to locating carcasses; it's what they do. If an elephant is shot, the vultures will be gathering at its carcass within minutes – the visibility chains pulling the birds in from miles around. It is this activity, this swarm of birds that can alert the anti-poaching teams. The vultures have unwittingly become the sentinels of the savannah. Unfortunately, these all-seeing sentinels are a threat to the poachers – they can't have the vultures telling the authorities what they are up to and so they seek to silence them, to stop the message from being broadcast. An animal carcass laced with a deadly poison called Carbofuran will kill hundreds of vultures in one hit. The poachers know this and so this is what they do. From their point of view, if they get rid of the vultures, they get rid of the threat of being discovered, the threat of being caught. The results are catastrophic: the birds that visit the carcass die, the chicks left alone on their nesting ledges die, entire colonies die.

A slow-breeding species like a vulture is simply incapable of quickly bouncing back from this sort of devastation. A breeding pair will only produce one chick per year, and that chick won't breed for many years. It will be a slow road to recovery if the poisoning stops; if the poisoning continues, it will be a fast road to extinction. In Extremadura, there is a slim possibility of seeing a Rüppell's Vulture in June, but at their current rate of decline there is a greater possibility of never seeing one anywhere other than in the pages of a book. The poisoning must stop or the Rüppell's will be lost forever.

Back out on the vast openness of the plain late in the afternoon, as the heat gradually begins to wane, I spot a couple of Black Vultures in one of the large fields. They look like two massive black rocks projecting out of the short, overgrazed turf. They are loafing – a term often used for waders when they rest up on estuaries, but equally as apt for these two vultures on the dry plains. They have fed recently and are letting the food go down, letting their digestive juices go to work. They look almost comical with their slightly hunched profile standing side by side, giving the impression of a couple of old men talking to one another in quiet voices at a funeral. A Black Kite flies by and diverts its flight path towards them to see if there is anything there for it, to see if the two vultures are an indication of food. It evidently doesn't see anything to hold its interest and it continues to fly on, flapping its long, sloped wings as it follows the ribbon of green that snakes its way through the parched turf.

It is now that the almost forgotten rains of March show their importance. The green ribbons delineate where unseen water flowed when the rain in Spain did indeed fall on the plain. It was almost three months ago that it last properly rained, but those rains are still giving life, still providing. The grass is still growing, sucking up the last of the moisture and attracting small birds, small mammals and large insects. The kite knows that the best feeding opportunity out here, away from a chance carcass, is to be found along these ribbons of life.

A Short-toed Lark scurries along the dusty edge of the track, pauses and then scurries some more. This is a dust-coloured bird for a dust-dominated environment and

Black Kites are abundant in the spring, patrolling the landscape and always alert to an easy meal.

its nondescript features are its one diagnostic feature. They are a common bird out here on the plains in the spring and summer months, but their small size, unobtrusive behaviour and colouration enable them to melt into the landscape so that they go largely unnoticed. This one is gathering up small insects to feed its young, which will be tucked away inside a delicate, intricately woven grass nest situated at the base of a grassy tussock. When a Black Kite drifts by overhead the lark squats down, a motionless mix of dull brown amidst a background of more dull browns. The kite never sees it.

Several Griffon Vultures punctuate the blue – all high, all drifting and all watching intently. A Short-toed Eagle sits atop one of the poles that delineate the route of a track across the plain; it appears too big for the pole and disproportionate in scale. The eagle's large head gives it a distinctive shape as it sits there motionless, watching the track, watching for a snake or lizard to carelessly cross the open space below, to carelessly and recklessly reveal its presence to this specialised predator. Several dainty Lesser Kestrels, which breed in a colony in a ramshackle, tumbledown collection of farm buildings not far from where I am standing, are feeding on the insects in the grassland, swooping down in fast plummeting movements and snatching them out of the grasses in graceful delicate manoeuvres. They are after the locust-like Egyptian Grasshopper, a huge insect up to seven centimetres long and packed full of protein; a meal in itself for a small falcon. The Lesser Kestrels love them, as do the Black Kites and the White Storks, several of which are walking slowly and purposefully on long legs wading through the grass, pausing to strike downwards with their huge orangey-red bills when the opportunity presents itself.

As you drive along the straight roads that cross the plains, it is easy to think of them as empty landscapes, devoid of interest. But the opposite is true; they are packed full of life, continuously busy with the everyday drama of survival. It is a harsh landscape, an unforgiving one, and the wildlife found within it is often very different from that found in the other habitats in Extremadura. There are many specialists – the bustards, the

Vast expanses of plains can often look empty, even the livestock are thinly scattered, but they are home to some fantastic birds.

sandgrouse and the ever-singing Calandra. I am here to see one such specialist, a bird that I have been completely entranced by all spring.

Montagu's Harriers are glorious birds – they don't fly through the air, they simply float. They move across the sky as if they were performing a ballet, unwittingly showcasing their grace and poise as they go about their daily lives. Montagu's are relatively common here, but their numbers are declining. You can't stop watching them as they quarter the ground below on their long slender wings. An adult male is a mixture of soft greys and black and is a beautiful mesmerising sight, but it can be trumped.

A small number of Spain's Montagu's are different from the norm, different from the pictures in the books. They are dark morphs – a dull-sounding term for what is most certainly not a dull-looking bird. Montagu's Harriers return to Spain in early April, but it wasn't until the middle of the month that I first saw this bird, a dark morph female. She is a beautiful, bewitching thing; see her once and you too will be under her spell. I watched her pair up with a male, watched her dance across the spring sky with him. However, it is the male that normally steals the show; the males that you can't take your eyes off. But not with this pair – she blew him completely off the stage. His was merely a supporting role.

Now with well-developed young in the nest, she is a busy bird, hunting the grassland repeatedly to feed her ever-demanding young. Busy she may be, but she is as graceful and as beautiful as ever. It doesn't take me long to spot her floating low over the undulating ground, her warm chocolate-coloured plumage standing out against the faded grass below. There is no white ringtail on this ringtail, just that warm smooth chocolate, and when she turns you get to see the paler underside to her primaries, with the barring visible on them. This paler part of the underwing accentuates the darker coverts to perfection. What a bird! She drops, snatches something – it could be another one of the grasshoppers – and then she is off, floating back across the landscape back to her nest and hungry young.

It is not long before I see her again – a nest of young chicks requires a lot of grasshopper-sized food parcels! She is flap, flap, gliding her way towards me, buoyant in the still air and I watch hypnotised by her beauty, by her grace as she gets nearer and nearer to me. Only when she reaches the fence line does she bank away from where I am standing transfixed, the light flashing off the underside of her wings, the beautiful yellow eye glowing like gold before me.

She is away, floating further and further from me as she doubles back over the field, searching every section. The distance between us may be increasing all the time, but all I can see is that yellow eye glowing out from its warm chocolate surround. That stunning eye tells me she is a full adult; her chicks are in experienced hands and have a very good chance of fledging successfully. Several seconds pass before I become aware that I am standing there looking at nothing. I turn around smiling broadly – no one can see me, there isn't another human for miles, but I wish there was. I have an overwhelming urge to say "Did you see that!" just so I can relive the experience again.

The air is full of bird song, Calandras dominate and I can hear the bubbling of Bee-eaters, the buzz of Zitting Cisticolas and the tumbling jangle of Corn Buntings. They are all there, but for now, just now, I see only her.

JULY

The road straightens out once you are out of the sweeping curves of the Salor valley and forms a straight line of tarmac running almost north to south across the plain, a black strip surrounded by the faded, sun-bleached greens and browns of the surrounding countryside. As soon as I am on this straight section I spot a Black Kite, flying parallel with me along the side of the road. With no traffic about, I slow down to watch it flying beside me, a fellow traveller of the road, its head pointing downwards, its eyes scanning the tarmac edge, the ditch and the verge, its wings adjusting all the time, the rudder-like tail twisting in deliberate movement, slowing it down, speeding it up, making sure it misses nothing. Further on, I can see another one doing the same. I am only making a short journey of a couple of dozen kilometres, but I will see more Black Kites on this section of road than I will cars. Roads are profitable places for these scavengers. Traffic is minimal, but sadly casualties are common – vast numbers of larks, Corn Buntings and sparrows continually fly low and criss-cross the tarmac or, especially the newly fledged Crested Larks, wander naively across it on foot.

The Kites are aware of this, and of the consequences, and they regularly patrol the roads to clean up the unfortunate. They start at first light, hoping to find a casualty of the night and they return on a regular basis throughout the day. Some decide to opt for a more

Vultures squabbling over a carcass out on the plains.

sedentary manner and find a handy roadside telegraph pole to sit on, waiting and watching for the inevitable.

I see the first Griffon Vulture heading arrow-straight across the sky, full of intent and purpose. I soon see a second and then a third doing the same. Lunch is being served somewhere out on the plain. I turn off the tarmac and onto one of the tracks, bumping across the cattle grid and enveloping the car in a swirling cloud of fine dust. As the dust settles, colouring the car a uniform dirty brown, I see more birds. The direction they are heading will not bring them close to the track, but with a bit of luck, they will be visible from the top of the rise in front of me. I drive onwards, up the track and across the parched landscape that is now so dry you can almost hear it gasping for water. Once over the rise, I stop the car. The dust dances, swirling all over the vehicle, before finally settling down and I jump out.

The heat hits me straight away, a physical hit knocking the breath out of me after the cool air-conditioned interior of the car. An Extremaduran summer is a harsh, hot arid affair. It says 38°C on the dashboard of the car and it isn't even the hottest part of the day yet. Summertime, but the living isn't easy. I grab my hat and my binoculars and scan about. I find the vultures on the ground some way off. They are feeding on what I presume to be a cow, but in the dust-laden haze and the melee of squabbling Griffons, it is difficult to tell for certain. I look around me for other birds, maybe a Bustard or Sandgrouse, but it is useless really because the haze on the plains at this time of day is like a shimmering lake of water – it drowns all beneath it, obscuring everything. I look down at the grasses beneath my feet and realise they are alive with a myriad of cricket species, leggy outsized insects as long as my thumb, if not longer, clambering over the parched stems in a manner reminiscent of a Harryhausen plasticine creation.

In the sky above the haze, I see more vultures heading in; the visibility chain in action once again. There are already a lot on the ground, but the binoculars magnify the haze as well as the view and I'm too far to see exactly what is going on. They are a long way off and the sun-baked plains are not the sort of place you want to be trekking across on foot in this heat. I step out of the furnace and back into the car; the iced bottle of water I brought with me a welcome relief.

I turn the car around and trundle back down the track across the scorched grasslands, past the cattle standing listlessly in the heat. Livestock deaths are very much part of the extensive farming culture out here. Anything weakened by disease or illness is very vulnerable to this heat, but anything that succumbs is quickly cleaned up by nature's very own clean-up crew. Vultures provide a service that is quick and efficient. By removing diseased animals, and destroying any bacterium and viruses present in the carcasses in their cast-iron gut, they prevent the spread of various diseases, from Bovine Tuberculosis to Rabies and even Anthrax. The vultures destroy these for breakfast, lunch and dinner.

Getting rid of carcasses officially is an expensive and time-consuming process – there are phone calls required, forms that need filling out, diseases to be checked for, bodies collected, loaded and driven away and then, finally, incinerated. The vultures bypass all

Vultures quickly gather at livestock carcasses, rapidly removing them and any disease threat.

this fuss, all this time and effort, and they do it for free. You would have thought that farming would welcome vultures, and, by and large, the actual farmers do. They recognise the valuable service that the vultures provide, they benefit from the sanitation cleansing that the birds carry out and they save time and money – lots of money – as a result. Yet, the farming industry also carries a lethal threat to this free efficient service, one that they don't even need to be carrying. Vested interests, big money and procrastinating politicians are putting these vultures in mortal danger.

One of the great vulture strongholds in the world is the Indian subcontinent in Asia. Or rather, it *was* one of the great vulture strongholds in the world. In the late 1980s, the vultures that lived there started to die in their hundreds, thousands, hundreds of thousands and, ultimately, in their millions. A few decades ago, the White-rumped Vulture, a close relative of the Griffon Vulture, was the most common large bird of prey on the planet, with their population numbering in the millions. Now, there are only about ten thousand adults left, and they are no longer common, they are Critically Endangered. Almost ninety-nine per cent of their population died in just twenty years. Other species have also suffered the same catastrophic declines – the Indian Vulture and the Slender-billed Vulture are now also listed as Critically Endangered, despite being common birds before the dying began.

The cause of this wholesale devastation? Not some crude poison, but a medicine, a medicine that you are highly likely to have taken yourself. The non-steroidal anti-inflammatory drug (NSAID) called Diclofenac is a widely used medication in human medicine and, unfortunately for the vultures, also in veterinarian medicine. It is a drug that is safe for us mammals to take, but it isn't safe for birds and it is absolutely lethal to vultures, particularly to those within the *Gyps* genus, such as the White-rumped and Griffon Vultures. It causes fatal kidney failure, even at very small doses. If a vulture ate cattle remains and only one per cent of the food consumed contained Diclofenac, it will be enough to kill the vulture.

Once the cause of what was killing the vultures of the Indian subcontinent was discovered – and it took an agonisingly long time to find it and reduced the vulture populations to the brink of extinction before the link was finally made in 2003 – the governments of India, Pakistan, Iran and Nepal banned the use of Diclofenac as a veterinarian product. The vulture population in this area has been devastated, but at least, at the very last minute, the source of this devastation has been stopped. A lesson learnt just in time you'd think.

The problem is that the lesson hasn't been learnt. Other countries haven't followed suit – they haven't banned Diclofenac as a veterinarian product and they are still marketing it to farmers in countries where vultures perform such a vital clean-up role in the landscape; countries like Italy, Portugal and Spain. It is still perfectly alright for Diclofenac to be used as a veterinarian product in these countries, even though these countries are home to well over ninety per cent of Europe's vulture population.

Despite heavy lobbying and vocal campaigning by several wildlife organisations, not to mention the overwhelming scientific evidence, the governments of Italy and Spain still haven't banned Diclofenac. The European Union won't remove the product's licence; however, some countries have shown common sense, for example France has banned it as veterinarian product. But the countries that *need* to ban it, that surely *have* to ban it, choose not to. Vested interests must be playing a part, there can be no other reason.

Alternatives exist. Alternatives that have the same veterinarian benefits as Diclofenac, with the only difference being that they don't kill vultures. Allowing this drug to still be licensed for use in livestock in areas where vultures are present means that the potential for a repeat of the Indian subcontinent disaster is still with us. At the moment, Diclofenac is not killing Europe's vultures and it isn't being used as readily as it was in Asia. This could be for economic reasons, but it could also be the way the product is marketed. However, markets and economics are always subject to change – surely we are not going to wait for this change, to wait for the vultures to die in their droves before we do the sensible thing.

Diclofenac is not the only veterinarian threat to vultures. The farming industry routinely pumps all sorts of drugs into livestock – in fact, it has become a norm of animal husbandry to do so. Antibiotics and antiparasitics, especially worming anthelmintics, are routinely used, and although their effects on the human food chain are not comprehensively known, their effects on scavenging wildlife, particularly on vultures, is hardly known at all. These drugs may well have sublethal effects in small doses, as did the organochlorine compounds that were widely used in agriculture following World War Two, which spread insidiously throughout the food chain and accumulated in many wildlife species until a tipping point was reached and the disastrous effects became evident in the 1960s. We just do not know. The Diclofenac disaster has at least made us aware of the potential dangers, and studies are now being carried out on various products that are readily available and are readily used. Some of the preliminary results are already sounding alarm bells. Lesions in the mouths and throats of young Black Vulture chicks in the nest in Andalucía are being linked to an antibiotic used in intensive farming systems, and the ability of Bearded Vultures to thermoregulate properly may be being compromised by a worming drug used in sheep. There are many other examples. Vultures are under threat like never before.

Vultures profit from death. It is a phrase so widely used it has become a sort of cliché. The human relationship with vultures is a complicated one. We don't like death, we shy away from it, we invent all sorts of fabrications to give us some form of comfort in the inevitable. And then we see vultures and they remind us of the harsh reality of living. Death. To those that don't know them, vultures may signify death, but to those that get to know them, they are simply an exhilaration. Many people think that these magnificent birds are something to be afraid of, that they are evil in some way, even though it has been shown time and time again that by removing carcasses rapidly and efficiently, vultures cleanse the environment and protect us, our livestock and wildlife from both disease and infection. We need to change the typical perception of what a vulture is – people not only need to know the benefits that these birds bring, but also the enjoyment.

It is hard to bird in this heat, in the traditional sense of the word. But then I guess it comes down to how you choose to bird. I am sitting with a friend at a table on a terrace underneath a massive shade-bearing canopy outside the hotel where my clients stay during the spring. The owner, another friend of mine, has just furnished us with another couple of ice-cold drinks and some tapas to enjoy, and we enjoy them as we sit there birding. Pallid Swifts are racing around the pantiled rooftops across the street, slicing through the air on their sickle wings. Common Swifts are present too, but not in the number that the Pallids are. They can be hard to separate, especially when in a bright sky, but when they drop below the skyline, as these ones are doing, you can see them in detail rather than as a blacked-out silhouette, their lighter colour becomes apparent and the contrast between the wings and the back is much easier to see.

The screaming swifts careering around the buildings and flashing by the rooftops have been entertaining us for several minutes, as has a Serin that has been rattling away in the tops of the trees that line the streets. He has proved tricky to see, keeping within the leafy green canopies and their shade, but we have had occasional glimpses of dazzling yellow every now and again, a real sunglasses-bird. A Black Redstart occasionally sings for us too, but it is half-hearted compared to its spring serenades. We spotted the male briefly, but have mainly seen the female as she flycatches around a small evergreen shrub growing in a small section of garden on top of a retaining wall, dashing off her perch and snapping her bill shut, snaffling insect after insect in the early afternoon sunshine.

Peering around the shade-bearing canopy above has given us many views of Black Kite in the air. They are abundant, seemingly everywhere now, and the birds that bred here in the spring are still here with their now-fledged and independent young. Their numbers have been augmented by wandering non-breeders and birds moving down from the north as they prepare for their migration south in just a couple of weeks. And above them, there are, of course, the vultures. There is always vulture traffic in the sky here, mainly Griffons, but the occasional Black and at least two Egyptian Vultures have drifted past since we have been here in this busy little town and we can watch these huge birds whilst we enjoy a drink and a bite to eat – that's how to bird in the heat.

After our refreshments, we head to the quarry on the other side of the tamed Tajo, exploiting the shade afforded us by the sheer rock walls. The deep, dark waters of the quarry are glass-like, reflecting the sky and the movements across it. The dark brown feathered chick ensconced in the Egyptian Vulture's nest is now almost ready to leave, to take its first flight and prepare rapidly for its forthcoming migration back to Africa. Fitting in a successful breeding cycle is a tight squeeze for the migratory Egyptian – they arrive at the end of February or beginning of March, they have to re-establish their territory, refurnish or even rebuild their nest, the eggs take forty-two days to hatch and then the chicks are in the nest for around one hundred days before they fledge, after which they are dependent on the adults for another thirty or so days and then they go, heading for Africa again at the end of September or beginning of October. That's a breeding cycle, from egg to independence, of roughly one hundred and seventy-five days jammed into a stay of around

The scruffy stick nest of an Egyptian Vulture

two hundred and fifteen days. There is no slack in the system for the Egyptian and this is no doubt one of the pressures on the bird that is leading some to remain here in this vulture landscape all year round.

The migratory Egyptian is dabbling at becoming a resident. Each year a small but significant number of birds don't attempt the migration back to Africa; they choose to remain in Extremadura instead. Overwintering individuals of the species have been recorded many times before, with one record for southern Spain from the 1870s, but in the last few years, there has been a steady increase in the number of birds that have seen out the colder months of the European winter.

In the winter they become gregarious, forming dormitories or winter roosts, which enables local conservationists to get accurate counts of the birds. The first complete overwintering was confirmed in the winter of 2008/2009, and in 2019 nearly one hundred birds were thought to be present in the region during the winter, the majority of which stayed in the area of the Tajo immediately to the north of where we are watching this chick. Most of these wintering birds are adults, but all age classes have been recorded. What isn't known is whether these birds are birds from the breeding population in Extremadura or whether they are from elsewhere in the country, or even further afield. What is known, however, is that these numbers are increasing slowly, year on year. It could be climate change, it could be an increase in new food sources that can be exploited throughout the whole year (the wintering birds are very fond of the new, very large, outdoor pig-rearing farms that have sprung up in some areas); it is most likely a combination of the two, but it is certainly interesting and it makes sense for these birds to stay if they are able to do so. Migration always comes at a cost – long arduous journeys take their toll. But overwintering also comes at a cost – the risk of poor weather, which negates the bird's ability to find food and feed, is a cost that most at the moment aren't willing to pay. But if that cost lessens, if it becomes less than the cost of migration, then the birds will favour it. Nature is always economical.

The young chick stares back at us with its beady, disinterested eyes as we watch it in its hollow in the rock face. The site's location seems unusual in that it is relatively low and easily observed at unusually close quarters, but at this time of year the location suddenly makes perfect sense – the hollow is bathed in shade, it doesn't get the full burning, relentless sun and the chick is protected by the vast, towering granite walls that surround it. A site well chosen. Suddenly the chick switches its attention from us, it becomes animated, looking up into the sky. We follow its gaze and see an adult bird that has just entered the airspace above this man-made hole in the ground. The chick is evidently excited at the prospect of what the adult is bringing back for it as it stands up unsteadily in the nest and begins to fidget about, all the time following the movement of the adult intently. The chick is obviously hungry, and to prevent our presence from putting the adult off, we slope quickly away, leaving the parent bird to come in and attend to its waiting offspring.

Back out on the access track, we look down towards the dammed Tajo, looking over a large forgotten area of land, dominated by leggy *Retama* scrub and rounded Evergreen

Oaks, interspersed incongruously with tall Eucalyptus trees and squat concrete creations, both alien reminders from the days of the dam building. A party of Azure-winged Magpies attracts our attention with their loud rasping calls. These are lovely corvids, delicate, long-tailed and beautifully hued with blue on the wings and tail. They are not immediately obvious, but then one flies from an Evergreen Oak into another tree, followed by a second bird then a third. Others follow, some leapfrogging the tree that the first three flew into, disappearing into the canopy of the next one instead. They are social corvids, gregarious crows, and form large, loose flocks of related birds. We watch them for several minutes moving across the landscape in front of us, a pastel-coloured stop-start of a flock. We try to count the birds as we watch them, but it is not easy – they are always on the move, but never all together, never moving at the same time. Eventually they move away from us, we can still hear their calls, but we can no longer see them flitting from tree to tree. I counted forty-three of them, my friend forty-five, so we'll say forty-four and call it quits. Despite that relatively large number, we probably never saw more than six or seven of them out in the open at any one time. They move in dribs and drabs, a trickle of birds rather than a flow, never exposing the whole flock. A small group will fly a short distance and then vanish into the thick, heavy branched canopy of an oak. After them another small group will move as well, sometimes bypassing the tree the others flew into, but always heading in the same general direction. At all times they are vigilant, a flock of many eyes, always on the lookout, alert to feeding opportunities and to danger, constantly calling and communicating with each other. There are plenty of predators here and this clandestine flocking is their way of avoiding exposure to it.

As if to reiterate that point, a compact-looking dark morph Booted Eagle glides purposefully over the trees; the white marks on the leading edge of the wings looking just like the headlights the bird books describe them as. Its purposeful flight signals its intent, an intent recognised by many birds as a chorus of alarm calls rise up from the oaks and scrub around us. These are efficient bird hunters, stocky and powerful, capable of surprisingly nippy manoeuvrings through trees as well as high-speed stooping. The magpies are right to be wary. A tag team of angry, vociferous Spotless Starlings rise up from the scrub, glossy black interceptors, individually mobbing the raptor, before quickly dropping back down again and allowing the next bird to have a go and buzz the threat. It is a clever tactic because it prevents the eagle from focusing on one bird. Just as one starling starts to annoy the eagle, it drops away and is replaced by another starling from a different angle. Clever and effective, the Booted Eagle chooses to forage elsewhere, flapping its wings to speed it away from the irksome, noisy starlings.

Ignoring all this activity below it, a Black Vulture serenely glides over on its huge wings, its large shadow blindly chasing after it over the tree-covered ground below. The massive wingspan, as wide as the track we drove along to get here, keeps the bird afloat on the sea of air, riding the air currents nonchalantly. The nearby huge concrete dam not only generates electricity, but it also generates a tremendous uplift of warm air, which creates more movement and disperses unseen rivers of air outwards across the terrain. It is these rivers of air that the Black is following by navigating their meanderings, sometimes having to turn back on itself, into an eddy of air to gain height without the exertion of flapping those long broad wings. A female can weigh over two stone in weight and yet she is able to float through the sky as if she weighed no more than one of her feathers. They are the epitome of efficiency.

The bird above us, majestic in its flight control, is an immature bird, probably one of last year's offspring. The plumage of the Black Vulture is, as its name suggests, very dark, but as the bird ages, as it reaches maturity around five years of age, the plumage lightens a tad, becoming browner, more faded in appearance. This bird, with its distinctive pale feet tucked up against the short wedge-shaped tail, is as black below as its name suggests.

Following the unseen highways of the sky, the bird effortlessly crosses the countryside laid out before us, getting further away from us every moment and seemingly shrinking before our eyes, until eventually becoming just a speck in the blue away to the south. It never flapped those mighty feathered sails once.

The three syllabled fluty note whistle that emanates from an elongated clump of tall, long-leafed, alien Eucalyptus below us, draws our eyes out of the blue and back down to the greens and browns of the ground. The sound is so clean, so clear and so distinctive that it cuts through the hot summer air. A beautiful, evocative, tantalising and often frustrating sound, it is the call of a Golden Oriole. With contrasting yellow and black colouration, a hazard warning sign of a bird, this bird is impossibly, brilliantly and perfectly camouflaged.

There is no breeze, but the air is always moving and these rivers of air used as vulturine highways tickle and tremble the long slender leaves of the eucalypts, the contrasting greens of the under and upper sides of leaves making the trees a shimmering sight with the moving shadows rippling through the canopy as each individual leaf moves in its own way. A flash of gold, pure unadulterated yellow searing its way along the trees – a male Golden Oriole out in the open long enough for us to really see it, to watch its sweeping, undulating flight as it speeds along on the black wings that accentuate the bright beauty of its head and body. It arcs up and into the green of the eucalypt and instantly vanishes, one of nature's conjuring tricks sublimely performed in front of us. We know where the bird is, we both saw it go in and land, we both study the spot intensely with our expensive optics, yet we can't see this bright yellow and black magician. We hear it though, clear and pure in tone as it whistles its signature across the airwaves.

We return to the quarry to the relative coolness of its shady depths. The young Egyptian Vulture with its head down is asleep in the nest, taking a siesta in the afternoon heat after its meal. There is no sign of the adult; it has headed out looking for more food for its chick. Unlike the Griffon and the Black, which typically lay just the one egg, the Egyptian normally lays a brood of two eggs about four days apart. The female starts to incubate as soon as the first egg is produced, which results in this first egg hatching three to five days before the second. The second chick is immediately placed at a disadvantage because it has to compete against the bigger and more dominant one for food and will invariably miss out on feeding until the larger, older chick is sated. In good years both chicks will be raised, but typically it is only one that will make it to fledging, with the other succumbing to starvation and the eventual ignominy of becoming a meal for its sibling.

Standing in the shade of the sheer rock walls we watch the small sandy shoreline of the quarry's water – the one place in the large quarry where the water isn't surrounded by vertical cliffs. Numerous small birds take advantage of the easy access to the precious resource to drink, bathe and enjoy its cooling presence as they send a myriad of small ripples chasing across the mirror surface. House and Spanish Sparrows dominate, noisily chattering and bickering amongst themselves, all hustle and bustle as they drink and bathe. A third species of sparrow joins the scene. Quieter, calmer and so much more unobtrusive in its behaviour. First one, and then two Rock Sparrows fly in, the white spots at the end of their tail feathers flashing in the shade as they fan them out to lose speed and land. They opt to drink from the far edge, away from the lively drama of the other sparrows, their boldly striped heads giving them a visual virtual Mohican as they stoop down to sip the water. More birds pour in and the species count goes up. Twittering Goldfinches and Linnets, flashy Serin, a lone Rock Bunting and several delicate Red-rumped Swallows all drop in to drink and to join the crowd, but they are nervous. Exposed and some way from cover, they are vulnerable and they sense it. A wave of uneasiness spreads throughout them. A mistaken alarm call from one of the sparrows causes a moment of panic, massed wings blurring, a split second of frenzied flight until the mistake is realised and they all settle back down again to continue their edgy drinking.

A Griffon Vulture drifting past in the blazing summer sky.

A Black Kite suddenly appears, flying low over the high quarry walls, the alarm calls sound from all quarters, the wings blur into motion again and everything scatters, seeking cover, seeking sanctuary. The water's edge is suddenly empty and devoid of birdlife; the Black Kite continues on its way, seemingly oblivious to the panic and turmoil it has just caused. The raptor crosses the water and eventually disappears over the far face of the quarry. The small birds don't immediately return, but they will have to because sources of accessible drinking water are in short supply at this time of year. They have no choice but to the run the gauntlet again and again, exposing themselves to danger, risking their lives for the life-giving water. By forming a mixed flock, they increase their chances of spotting a predator early – many eyes and ears all tuned to danger – but conversely, they also increase the chance of attracting the hungry interest of the predators – concentrations of potential meals don't go unnoticed. Inevitably it is the Spanish Sparrows that return first. The noisy gregarious behaviour, at first subdued, slowly and predictably comes to the fore again. The females are identical, to our eyes at least, to the females of the House Sparrow, but the males are distinctive and much more gaudy in appearance with their chocolate brown head, clean white cheeks and bold black bib and breast. Their incessant noise reassures the other small birds who begin to slowly, cautiously, return.

Watching the small birds slake their thirst makes us realise our own and we return to the town to enjoy a much-needed liquid refreshment. Shrieking, screaming swifts continue to dash around the rooftops, blazing between houses at breakneck speed, but overhead, above us and above the swifts, the vultures continue to drift by.

AUGUST

Desiccated and devoid of moisture, the land is exhausted by the aridity of the long punishing summer. Mini, self-generated, whirling dervish dust tornados spontaneously spin into life before burning themselves out across the open, exposed plains. Great Bustards blur and break up in the wavy sea of heat haze that has drowned the parched land. Everything struggles, every bit of shade is valued, utilised. Fence posts, which in spring provided perches for Corn Buntings, now provide a thin slither of shade for the birds to sit in on the ground. The heat is on. For several days the thermometer has marched forcibly into the forties. The cloudless month of August is the month that puts the extreme in Extremadura.

It is too much for some. Several of the spring and summer visitors have already left – the abundant Black Kites of the last five months have gone, the dazzling blue Rollers too and White Storks, such an avian emblem of the area, have moved off to the irrigated rice-growing areas in the south. But the vultures remain. The heat takes its toll on the wildlife and the livestock in the area and the vultures gather to clean it up, seemingly immune to the heat, impervious to it. They are not, of course, but they are perfectly adapted to cope with it. These most efficient flyers turn out to be thermo-efficient too.

Despite the all-encompassing heat of August, you won't see a Griffon Vulture seeking the shade, they seem to be just as comfortable out on the shade-less plain as they are on a ledge in a shadowy quarry. The secret to this ability to cope with the heat is broadly the same as their ability to cope with the cold: feathers. It is thought that the dinosaurs, and let's not forget that birds are their modern-day descendants, first evolved feathers as a form of insulation to help keep their body temperature at the required level. Managing temperature evolved long before flight did.

But although feathers hold the secret to how these birds keep cool in the heat of the summer, it is not their actual presence that is key; instead it is the lack of them. Griffon Vultures have surprisingly large areas of bare skin on their bodies, by exposing this skin, and therefore the network of blood vessels immediately beneath it, the vultures can allow their body heat to escape. It is a process known as thermoregulation, a process that the Griffons are very adept at.

Partaking in the pastime of vulture watching allows you to see this strategy in action. Watch a Griffon on a ledge in August and you will see a bird with an obvious long neck and a flattened collar of a ruff, which appears to have the top button undone to reveal a V-shape gap in the feathers at the top of the bird's chest. The bird's bare lower legs will also be visible,

A thermo-regulating Griffon Vulture can expose a third of its body surface to the air to help maintain its cool.

exposed to the cooling movement of the air. But see the same bird on the same ledge in the chilled air of January and the impression is very different – the bird is all hunched up, looking as if it has hardly any neck at all, and the flattened collar of the summer is now a resplendent fluffed up ruff. You won't be able to see the bare legs because the feathers of the undercarriage cover them completely. The only bare area exposed to the winter air is the bird's head. By changing the amount of skin exposed, the bird can manage its body temperature effectively and efficiently. It has been estimated that by merely adjusting its posture, a Griffon Vulture can change the amount of bare skin exposed from just seven per cent of its body surface to thirty-two per cent. In other words, when it is as hot as it is now in August, a Griffon Vulture can expose almost one-third of its total body surface to the air, allowing its internal body temperature to dissipate.

The key to thermoregulation is all about how the bird holds itself – posture and deportment are key to the Griffon's ability to deal with the challenge of extreme temperatures. Evolution, as always, proves to be the ultimate finishing school.

All of this, however, goes against the widely held belief that vultures have bare necks and bare heads because of how they feed, to avoid feathers getting gummed up with bodily fluids and viscera as they plunge their heads and necks inside the carcass. Although the lack of feathers is undoubtedly cleaner for the bird, it is now apparent that this is only a secondary benefit; the primary evolutionary driver for the bare neck and head of the Griffon Vulture is not about feeding, it is about being cool.

The Turkey Vulture, which is found throughout most of the Americas, has another adaptation to help it keep cool in the summer heat. It urinates on itself. Bird droppings are a mixture of both faeces and urine, and Turkey Vultures, as well as some species of stork, deliberately vent this mixture on to their legs in hot weather. The baking sun of summer evaporates the fluids in the droppings from the bare scaly surface of the bird's legs, producing a cooling effect known as urohydrosis. This can lead to the legs of the birds that practice this form of thermoregulation being stained with characteristic white streaks, which are from uric acid crystals that have been left behind after the liquid in the urine has evaporated. Vultures waste nothing.

Noel Coward's most famous quote about the mad dogs and Englishmen is a warning. A warning that I heed. I venture out for a walk around the village's reservoir, not in the mid-day sun, but in the early morning sun. It is still hot, but the burning, roasting heat of the middle of the day is still to come. Everything seems listless and limp, there is no breeze to move the trees, the scorched vegetation hangs motionless along the side of the track, the remnants of grass in the overgrazed fields no more than a faded, torn, thinly veiled covering for the dust like soil beneath.

A young Griffon Vulture showing the bare neck and head, a feature evolved for thermoregulation rather than cleanliness.

The reservoir is dwindling fast; its island is now a peninsula reunited with the mainland again. Large expanses of crazy-paved baked mud surround what's left of the water. The marginal vegetation that was so lush and full of promise in the spring is now nothing more than a dried-up stranded line of withered stems, demarcating where the water once reached. Despite this, life still goes on. Dazzling dragonflies hawk through the air, Crested Larks continue to scurry across the track's dusty gravel surface and a Grey Heron stands motionless by the water's edge, an elegant grey and white statue placed between the dry, cracked mud and the flat, green water. A male Stonechat clicks and ticks away at me from a fence post before dropping down into cover and, as I walk on, a previously unseen Hoopoe suddenly rises from the track edge, its cryptically disruptive zebra-like camouflage disguising it right up to the moment it took to the air, flying away from me on its beautiful butterfly wings.

A Black Vulture glides overhead with no apparent particular purpose and I think back to the youngster I watched in its giant nest almost two months ago. It will have fledged now, finally leaving the confines of the nest to fly liberated through the air, gradually starting on its road to independence in this vulture landscape.

I pause momentarily to take a much-needed slug of water from my bottle. As I do so, I look back towards the village, the white-washed walls gleaming in the light, and I spot a large bird heading towards me and the reservoir. It's a raptor and the long-winged, gull-like silhouette is at once distinctive. An Osprey. The fish-eating raptor is making its long journey from the north to the south and has evidently decided to take a break en route, dropping down in altitude to see what opportunities it can find. It seems a strange time of year for a bird, which in Britain we associate with the colder mountainous terrain of Scotland, to turn up and spend some time in one of the hottest regions in Europe.

It flies over the reservoir, carefully studying the water below, gliding on angled wings. Suddenly it banks away, turning sharply in the air to retrace its route. It flaps heavily and laboriously as it hovers over the water; something has evidently caught its attention and I stand there spellbound, hoping that I am going to see this magnificent aerial fisherman plunge downwards and snatch a fish. I am to be disappointed though because whatever first caught its attention only holds it for a few seconds more and then the bird moves on, over the water and then the perimeter track, before switching course slightly and heading for a nearby reservoir a couple of kilometres to the south.

I have seen Ospreys catch countless fish on television programmes, spectacular shots of the bird thrusting its legs forward as it crashes into the surface of the water, rising again, long wings spraying huge droplets in large arcs as it emerges with a large fish tightly gripped in its specialised feet, sharp talons spearing through the scales of its prey. However, it is a sight I have never seen in the flesh, so to speak, and one I would dearly love to see. Just for a moment, a brief but exhilarating moment, I thought that this was going to be it, but alas no. My luck could still be in though; Ospreys on migration often stop in these parts for several weeks, taking an extended break in their migratory ramble. I can only hope that I will be in the right place at the right time.

Looking out over the reservoir it is easy to see why the Osprey is visiting this hot dry region, the Spanish are keen fishermen and, as a result, many reservoirs are stocked with a wide variety of large fish, many probably too big to be caught by the Osprey, but there will be plenty that are the right size. Now, with the water level dropping rapidly, the once wide, deep expanses of water are becoming ever more concentrated into narrower and shallower pools. The fish within them are forced to swim nearer the surface as they compete for space and oxygen, becoming metaphorical sitting ducks and allowing the Osprey to take its pick.

Where Extremadura meets Portugal in the bulge of land below the Tajo river, the air is always a little bit cooler and the slight climb in altitude brings a modicum of relief from the searing summer temperatures. The hills are covered in pine plantations, criss-crossed with a network of fire breaks forming random geometric patterns amongst the monochromatic green of the trees. Towering rocky outcrops cap the tops of the hills, vertebrae-like mounds ripping through the skin of trees below. These strange-looking formations provide a home for the Griffon Vultures, giving them a secure nesting and roosting site from where they can launch their daily feeding forays. The immediate pine-dominated landscape might not offer much in the way of feeding opportunities for them, but these birds often fly up to four hundred kilometres a day in their search for food. They are therefore only a short commute from the boulder-strewn farms that fringe this tree-growing area, and a few kilometres more takes them over the cork-producing dehesas of the Sierra de San Pedro, with the vast open plains around the Salor also well within their range.

The relative coolness of the area and the abundance of tree-cast shade make this the countryside to be out in during August. The clean smell of the pines brings a freshness lacking elsewhere and it is a serene and tranquil place, but it is by no means a quiet one. A constant ragged chorus of noise fills the air emanating from all around you, each tree playing host to several sources, sources that somehow manage to follow their own individual rhythm and never following the same pattern. Cicadas, B-movie looking Homopteran bugs, are all around, clinging to the stems and branches of the trees, drumming out their high decibel din. The relentlessness of the noise eventually allows you to gradually tune it out until, somehow, you forget they are there.

Alpine Swifts arc across the blue sky in tight formations, flashing their white undersides as they do so. A young Short-toed Eagle, newly fledged, is flying slowly over the slopes of young pines, over the serried ranks of the next generation of timber. It is still being fed by its parents but, impatient for a meal, it has taken to the wing and is aimlessly flying about awaiting their return. Comfortably confident with the newly discovered skill of flying, the young bird drifts further to the right, picks up an updraft and swings around towards a clump of mature trees, unwittingly straying into protected airspace.

An indignant, intolerant Hobby, affronted by the intrusion so close to where its own young are perched in the branches of their nest tree, darts upwards from the dark green uniformity of the pines, flooding the air with a splenetic fury of high-pitched calls as it dashes towards the hapless eagle. Talons flash across the face of the inexperienced youngster as the screaming falcon hurtles past. The eagle wobbles in the air, its long, broad wings flapping to stabilise it once again. The Hobby reaches the peak of its ascent, folds its wings and stoops, hurtling back down to attack once more. Unnerved by the assailing, raging aggressor, the larger bird tries to outmanoeuvre the agile, sleek Hobby. It has no chance, a cumbersome heavy bomber of a bird in comparison to the high-speed jet fighter falcon. A glancing blow across its long tail feathers sends the eagle into a dive, desperate to escape. Confused by the smaller bird's combative behaviour, it folds its big wings back, diving away over the young pines, unsure of where it is going, just wanting to put distance between itself and the falcon.

The Hobby pulls out of its dive, using the rapid momentum to climb again, racing up-wards through the sky, but this time it doesn't stoop. It can see the vanquished trespasser flee-ing below and, instead, the bird opens its wings and soars in a tight circle, calling once more, before descending back to the trees. The young Short-toed Eagle was no danger to the falcon's chicks, but the Hobby is a fiercely over-protective parent, one that sees all raptors as a potential threat – it couldn't allow the juvenile snake hunter to fly so close to its own precious brood.

A male Blue Rock Thrush potters about on a small protrusion of granite before ascending to the summit and striking the bird's characteristic pose of holding its head slightly cocked and angling the distinctive long bill upwards. Unlike the high tempo falcon, the Blue Rock Thrush is now unshackled from the bonds of parenthood; its brood have all fledged and are independent, affording this beautiful bird time to relax in its surroundings. A dweller of rocks, the bird's name is apt, its blueness highlighted by the strong sunlight as it once again potters over the granite, stopping every now and then to eye the crevices intently, looking for an insect or two to eat.

High above, and in a completely different world to the thrush, three Griffon Vultures fly, one after another, through the blue, following the same path back along the face of the cliffs, their broad wings held out from their bodies as they glide on the current of air. Others are sitting on the rocks, their long necks extended, exposing the bare skin to the air to help control their body temperature. The first of the three flying birds peels away to its right, away from the cliffs, tilting itself to bank in a wide arc until it is heading straight back towards the granite massif. Once lined up, it lowers the legs, breaks the flow of air over its streamlined body and descends to land with aplomb on one of the ledges. The second and third birds follow respectively, but the third lands too close to the first, forcing it to take avoiding action, shuffling off the ledge and back in to the air amidst harsh sounding utterances of discontent from both birds.

Was it a misjudgement by the third bird or was it a calculated manoeuvre by a more dominant individual over its subordinate? The answer presents itself as the bird that was forced to take to the air again, circles out away from the ledges, gaining enough height to once more drop onto the rock. This time though, it lands further away from the others, on a ledge by itself, a less prime piece of rocky real estate. Pecking orders apply to roosting ledges and this bird was just reminded of its place.

I soon enter the relaxing world of vulture gazing once again, observing the seemingly perpetual movement of vultures along these rocky outcrops; arrivals and departures, birds gliding by, birds sitting watching. I am not sure how long I stand there gazing – the warmth of the August day, the effortless movements of the Griffons and the underlying sound of the cicadas all have a deeply soporific effect on me and gradually reality recedes.

A loud laugh rudely interrupts my drowsiness and I look confusedly behind me, expecting to see someone standing amongst the neatly spaced trunks, but nobody is there. The laugh rings again through the trees, this time my gradually awakening brain recognises it for what it is: an Iberian Green Woodpecker. This very close relative of the Green Woodpecker has only recently been recognised as a separate species and has a restricted range in Extremadura. It is largely absent from the majority of the region, but here, where Spain bulges into Portugal, it is found in good numbers. Walking amongst the tall uniform trunks, I soon locate the laughing bird, but only see it briefly as it peers around one of the thick pine trunks to take a look at me before it scuttles back around the back of the tree. I hear it climb higher; its specialised climbing feet scratches up the bark's surface before it takes to the air, bounding away from me in the characteristic undulating flight of the woodpeckers and displaying the yellow rump like a bouncing tennis ball through the trees.

A Short-toed Treecreeper flies to the base of a pine a few metres away and begins its slow methodical climb upwards, probing the crevices and under the bark flakes with its bill, occasionally pausing to eat what it finds as it scales the tall branchless trunk. When it reaches the first horizontal branch it walks nonchalantly along the underside as if gravity was just a myth, the bird's sharp claws holding it fast. It gives up on the branch, letting go and dropping down to the bottom of a neighbouring pine, it begins its steady ascent once again. A roving party of Long-tailed Tits, a darker subspecies compared to the birds in Britain, fly past, moving through the trees in ripples that match their rippling flight calls as they do so, long tails following them as they go. The shady, cooler environment under the pines is alive with small birds; the dry heat more bearable beneath the luxuriant needle growth above. Linnets, Serin and Goldfinch scour the woodland floor searching for seeds beneath the sparse grasses. Further off, a Blackbird scatters the carpet of dry brown pine needles in the hope of finding a juicy morsel. These birds don't stop for a siesta; they have to get on with living.

I meander my way through the pines, occasionally getting inadvertently close enough to a cicada to cause it to stop its incessant racket. When they do suddenly fall quiet, the silence is almost deafening in its intensity, making you realise just how noisy it has been. But it is only a short reprieve; the bug chorus restarts almost immediately and the noise becomes the norm once more. I gradually make my way to the edge of the trees where I begin to feel the heat radiating off the fire break in front of me as I get nearer to it. I should stay within the trees, within their cooler interior, but I want to watch vultures and I won't find them in here.

The Griffon Vultures are arranged along the high rocky ridge several hundred metres in front of me, feathered gargoyles along the cathedral-like cliffs, watching all around them in their characteristically unworried way. I make my way slowly along the edge of the pines, carefully keeping in the shade as I go until I find an inclined trunk, just perfect to

Griffon Vultures, living gargoyles on the towering cliffs.

lean against. There are a few Griffons in the air and I watch three of them as they fly slowly along the sunburnt ridge. The trio pick up on an upward air current, hot air spiralling, fuelled by the heat reflecting back from the bare rock faces below. The birds gain height rapidly with their normal consummate ease and, as they do so, they attract the attention of some of the birds on the ledges below.

Long necks are craned upwards, the gaze fixed on the climbing birds, trying to read the significance of what the other vultures are doing. Decisions are rapidly made, two of the Griffons step off the ledge, entering the air flow, broad wings fully open, primaries splayed, inclined upwards. They begin to rise almost immediately and, as they do so, more follow. One, then two, then three and then four birds step into the air following the first two upwards. The remainder of the vultures on the cliff decide against following them, preferring to continue their gargoyle-like repose instead. It may be that they are still digesting food from earlier or, perhaps as they watched the first birds soar upwards, they read no significance in what those birds were doing.

Griffon Vultures are doing well in Spain, very well. The population is recovering from years of widespread persecution towards raptors and predators in general, and it is now clear that, until about 1960, the numbers of Griffon Vultures in the Iberian Peninsula were heavily suppressed by this persecution. However, in more enlightened times and with stricter wildlife protection laws in place, the Griffon has bounced back, taking full advantage of the abundant feeding opportunities and nest sites that the country has to offer. The booming population has led to many new colonies forming and the competition for nest sites is increasing. Griffons require steep inaccessible cliffs with plenty of ledges on which a colony can build their nests and lay their eggs. They also need the ledges to be away from human disturbance and, although Spain has an abundance of these type of sites, there are not an infinite supply of them.

In recent years, there has been an increase in the numbers of Griffons beginning to look elsewhere for their nest location. These huge raptors nest early and can lay claim to sites ahead of other species. A small number of tree nests belonging to Black Vultures and

Spanish Imperial Eagles have been taken over by usurping Griffons as the early breeding vultures explore different nesting options.

There are many other large bird species that have similar requirements to the Griffon Vulture when it comes to nesting on rocky cliffs, and they too can find that their nesting sites attract the Griffon's attention. I have known Black Stork, Egyptian Vulture and Eagle Owl all lose nest sites to the bigger bird. The dispossessed birds are then forced to move to other sites instead of their original preferred option.

This colonial behaviour explains the antipathy that other large birds can sometimes show towards the Griffon Vulture. Cliff nesters such as the Black Stork, Egyptian Vulture and Eagle Owl may be too small to successfully see off the vulture, but the Golden Eagle is not. Golden Eagles hold territory all year around and they react instantly and furiously to any Griffon that they deem to be taking too close an interest in their nest site. Griffons may be bigger than the Golden, but they don't have the lethal armoury, the sheer speed or the outright aggression of the eagle. Any interest they might have shown in an eagle's eyrie is very quickly forgotten when the owner hurtles towards them talons first.

I take a long drink of now tepid water from my bottle and decide to walk up the path to the pass, which is mostly in broken shade. The track goes arrow-straight through a section of younger pines, the un-thinned trees creating tall walls of green either side of the hard,

The Griffon Vulture's large size allows it to dominate some of the other birds that share its habitat.

stone track. Lizards scatter stones down the short steep bank that separates the trees from the path, scurrying bursts of activity as they propel themselves away from me as I walk slowly along. Tiger Beetles, little green jewels glinting in the dappled shade of the path, run across the stony surface at speeds that seem reckless in the heat. The chitinous click of dragonfly wings draws my attention to the presence of these other insect jewels, beautiful red colours buzz up and down the track edge, their supreme aerial skills as dazzling as their colour scheme.

The pines suddenly subside as the track meets the spot where the rocky, irregular ridge dips downwards, creating a bite-shaped gap in the skyline. A wooden open-sided shelter has long stood at this point and the deep shade it gives is as welcome as the breath of breeze that greets me as I stand at the top of the pass. From here one can appreciate how narrow the ridge is as it runs away on either side of me – a rock-strewn, jagged crease in the landscape, separating the pines of the border country from the dehesa of the interior. A group of Alpine Swifts scream their way through the pass in a black and white dash above my head, chasing each other around the ridge in energetic fashion, cutting through the air on their long, narrow, curved wings. The land in front of me falls away quickly and the initial Cistus-dominated slope is replaced by small grazing fields as the gradient eases before the sea of oaks take over. The dehesa is ringed by the Sierra de San Pedro in the west, which form a wall of hills swinging to the south, and ending in an old fortified castle town standing proud in the distance, the crenulations of its walls just visible through the binoculars.

Dozens of Griffons are in the sky in front of me, some flying back towards the ridge, others flying away from it, a sky full of vulturine traffic. A long way below, a Booted Eagle glides over the spreading canopies of the Cork Oaks travelling at speed and with menace as it jinks between the trees and disappears from my view. The immediate ridge is busy with Crag Martins and Red-rumped Swallows, and a Black Redstart dashes out on regular fly-catching missions whilst a less obvious Rock Bunting methodically makes its way over a large fallen boulder jammed into a fissure in the rock wall of the ridge. As my eye becomes more accustomed to the irregular shapes of the ridge, I begin to spot Griffons perched up on ledges and rocky promontories, taking in the same view as I am, but seeing so much more.

A movement in the glossy Cistus scrub below reveals a group of Red Deer hinds and their young calves slowly picking their way through, their heads popping up through the green canopy, chewing faces looking all around, eyes, ears and nose all alert to danger before popping back down into the scrub to continue feeding. They finally pick up my scent and three heads shoot up together as they stare towards me, the chewing stops and they focus all their senses on the scruffy wooden shelter in which I am hiding from the sun. Other heads appear with nervous twitches of the ears and staring eyes before they decide to move down the slope and away from what they have detected. I hear their hooves clicking across the stony ground and see the Cistus moving as they move through it, a controlled trot through the scrub until they reach safer ground away from my scent drifting in the air.

The Bonelli's Eagle exudes power in flight and when perched.

I watch the deer through my binoculars as they resume their sub-canopy grazing that is interspersed with periscope looks about. There are occasional nervous glances back to the pass at first, but I am soon forgotten and they move slowly away from me along the lower slope of the ridge before they melt away into the folds of the landscape. I redirect my binoculars out over the dehesa in front of me, watching several Griffons in the burning bright sunlight. But it is the straight trailing wing edge of another gliding raptor that catches my eye – an adult Bonelli's Eagle is in the air and gliding with intent along the ridge. These are powerful birds and are fearsome hunters with huge feet and proportionally massive talons. The rear one, often colloquially known as the killing talon, can be bigger than the Golden Eagle's, despite the fact that the Bonelli's is roughly two-thirds the size of its huge congener.

The white patch of plumage on the bird's back is evident as it starts to bank around and pick up some upward-moving air. I am unsure as to whether the bird is hunting or patrolling its territory. They feed on a wide variety of birds, mammals and reptiles, utilising several different hunting techniques and it could be that this bird is getting height to stoop at prey or it could be getting height to continue its patrol. Bonelli's always fly with purpose, exuding power no matter what the reason for their flight. This eagle gains height, but soon disappears behind the wall of rocky ridge running to my left. I scan about hoping to find this truly rapacious hunter again, but am unable to locate it.

A couple of Black Vultures are higher, much higher, and are flying together on their broad wings, small rectangular silhouettes against the blue. Much lower down, at roughly the same altitude as me, a young Black Vulture, probably a newly fledged bird, jet black, gliding on slightly drooping wings, is flying over the dehesa, heading in my direction. It is some way off when I first spot the huge dark shape against the far-off background of hills, but the river of air that it is riding is a rapid one and it soon becomes clear that this giant bird isn't just heading in my direction, it is heading straight at me. I am tucked in just under the roof of the shelter, my back against one of the supporting posts and I stand stock-still, not daring to move, as the vulture gets closer and closer. All the time I expect it to bank around, turn away from me, but it doesn't, it just keeps coming straight towards me, intent on the path that it is following through the sky, a path that evidently crosses the ridge at the small pass where I am standing.

Closer and closer it comes; my binoculars are now superfluous. With my eye I can now clearly see the black fuzz of down covering its head and face and the pale blue colour of the cere separating the face from the darkness of the bill tip. I see its eye staring straight ahead as the immense vulture flies right over me, filling me with unnerved exhilaration as the noise of the air shearing over its wings makes me want to duck down as the bird passes within metres of my head. The bird's enormous size dwarfs me as I stand rooted to the spot; three metres of dark black wingspan blotting out the blue sky – a vulture total eclipse.

SEPTEMBER

There is a freshness in the air, clouds of white wisps form in the blue for the first time in months, they dissipate quickly, but their very presence hints at the change in seasons. The ground responds to the moistening dew formed by the cooling night-time temperatures and a mini spring of small flowers appears on the plains, in the fields and on the road verges. Birds start to sing again, it's like a collective sigh of relief, another summer survived. Sometimes the white wisps, instead of vanishing, merge together, forming larger, greyer masses and brief showers of big drops fall from the sky bringing a hint of dampness to the ground below. The showers don't last long, but they still produce the first tangible rainfall for months.

The countryside echoes to the roar of the deer rut – the loud, guttural voices of the stags rolling through the dehesa and reverberating up the valleys, whilst the quieter, bleating, plaintive calls of this year's young, born in the spring, are an emotional counterpoint to the testosterone-fuelled bellows of their fathers. These Red Deer calves have suddenly found that their calm, steady existence has been shattered. There is confusion in the herds, the hinds are scattered by the males and inevitably some of the young get lost, bewildered by the abrupt change in mood. They are calling for their mothers, calling to be restored to the fold.

A Red Stag in the rut is an imposing beast, its muscular body in peak condition, topped off with a rack of fearsome, tined antlers. Occasionally, the males lock these antlers with others, grappling for dominance, but most of the time the males avoid full blown conflict, asserting their dominance with body language and their bellowing calls. They will fight if they have to, but it is a massive risk to take, antlers have evolved to push hard against other antlers, but a slip or a misjudgement can turn them into flesh-ripping weapons. In our own world of healthcare and antibiotics we forget that even a small wound can be a mortal one.

A large expanse of dehesa spreads over the undulations of the land between the village and the Salor river. It is home to many Red Deer and the rut is in full swing as I drive amongst the trees, bumping along the twisting track as it snakes between them. Eventually, the track deteriorates beyond the capabilities of my car and I leave it in the shade of an oak and continue on foot, stags are bellowing somewhere nearby, but the only deer I have seen so far have been a few hinds and their bewildered-looking calves.

After the stifling heat of the last two months the air feels cooler and freer, birds are more apparent, more active, taking advantage of the fresher conditions and the mini spring of growth in the plants and the insects they bring with them. Pied Flycatchers suddenly

Dehesa dominates large parts of the vulture landscape.

abound, they adorn almost every tree as if someone has scattered them in wanton abundance across the dehesa, they are here for only a few weeks, enjoying an extended break in their journey from northern Europe down to sub-Saharan Africa. The abundance of new insect life is an unmissable opportunity for these small black and white passerines on their trek south, flashing their wings as they dash from the branches, hovering momentarily as they snap their bill around their winged prey before flying back to the confines of the canopy to enjoy their little packet of protein. Fly-catching flycatchers doing exactly as their name suggests.

The managed oaks of the dehesa suddenly start to thin out, creating large grassy gaps and then, over a brow of a low ridge, a relic of our industrial past begins to appear. The broken ruins of a community of workers stand incongruously in the otherwise natural-looking landscape around me. The Salor valley was once home to a thriving gold mine and these ruins in front of me are all that is left of the workers' barracks and communal buildings that would, many decades ago, have been the focal point of so many people's lives. There was gold in them there hills.

The buildings in front of me are now long-forgotten shells of what they once were. Many of the roof timbers, like the labyrinth of shafts beneath the ground's surface, have been mined to exhaustion, but in this case, the excavations have been carried out by insect miners as opposed to human ones. The network of tunnels burrowed by decades of boring beetle larvae have caused many to collapse, the weight of the terracotta roof tiles above proving to be too much for the hollowed-out timbers that held them. The windows have long gone, as have the doors, no doubt recycled in newer buildings long before anyone had heard of architectural salvage. The gaping holes left behind by their removal adding to the eerie air that we tend to associate with old, uninhabited and dilapidated buildings.

But eeriness is simply a human concept; to the wildlife of the immediate area these broken buildings are an opportunity. A male Black Redstart sits atop a small, broken chimney singing proudly, his white wing panels almost glowing in the sunlight against his blackish grey upper body. There are an almost infinite number of nest sites amongst these structures for these beautiful little birds; his is a territory worth singing about. Numerous yellow Serin glow magnificently amongst the long grass stems that form little mazes through what were once pathways, the little finches gleaning the dusty slate surface for small seeds. The red faces of Goldfinch peer out from clumps of fearsome-looking thistles as they harvest the abundant downy seeds from the old flower heads. Spotless Starlings, all glossy iridescence, chatter away idly in the unkempt, straggly branches of what would have once been proudly pruned ornamental Honey Locust trees.

Black Redstarts are common breeding birds throughout the vulture landscape, at home in the heart of towns as they are in the countryside.

I spot a male Common Kestrel on the crumbling concrete ledge of a small window on the side of a little squat, square outbuilding. He glances at me briefly as if to acknowledge my presence before reverting to complete indifference. Like the Black Redstart, these buildings offer a wealth of breeding sites for the small and feisty falcon, but breeding is over and he seems to be intent on relaxing, the window ledge offering him the perfect place to do so. I walk along the old slate pathway that leads to the main entrance of the largest building, the scattered droppings of deer across the surface indicating that it isn't just the birds that feel at home here now.

I peer cautiously through the door aperture, eyeing the broken roof immediately above. It seems secure and so I step forward into a long narrow hallway, stepping onto the rubble remains of yesteryear. Another doorway on the left leads into a large room, still with its roof intact save for a few small holes through which the sunlight drops down in narrow columns to the dusty floor below. These small shafts of light emphasise the darkness within, a gloomy shroud obscuring the detail of the room. It takes a moment for my eyes to adjust from the bright light outside to the shadowed interior and when they do I find myself looking at a white ghost silently gliding across the room.

The kestrel isn't the only aerial predator to have made these old ruins its home; my white ghost is super nature rather than supernatural. A Barn Owl, glowing white, perches further back in the gloom and turns its heart-shaped face towards me to stare back at my intrusion with its beady black eyes. Not wishing to cause any undue disturbance, nor wishing to stand beneath the shattered roof any longer, I turn around and head back outside, sitting down on an old stone block and reliving the sight of the owl as it drifted silently across the room away from me.

Barn Owls in Extremadura are birds that are often found in urban areas. I hear their strange hissing, rattling call often as I lie in bed at night, as well as occasionally getting glimpses of them gliding over the narrow house-lined streets, their white underwings flashing in the arc of the streetlights as they silently hunt their prey. In the villages and the towns, they often feed on the roosting sparrows and starlings, but out here amongst the ruins, I imagine that the various small mammals that also call it home inadvertently find themselves on the menu of this stealthy night-time predator.

A noisy flock of Spanish Sparrows, tightly packed, swings between the buildings, the bright white cheeks of the males flashing in the sunlight as they all turn as one; House Martins glide overhead, interspersing their leisurely flight with rapid spurts of blurry wing beats as they pick insects out of the blue. I get to my feet, prompting an unseen Sardinian Warbler to loudly admonish me as I do so, and decide to move on, leaving the censuring warbler and the old broken buildings behind me as I continue my walk downwards, following the old stone track that heads into the valley and towards the old mine workings. The stones that pave my way are beginning to be subsumed by the grasses and other vegetation growing impertinently between them, their smooth polished surfaces reflecting the hard use they would have once had.

As the slope begins to steepen, so the vegetation changes once more. Cistus scrub and lavender, their scents hanging in the air, start to dominate, and with their domination come the harsh calls of Dartford Warblers. Here and there wild Olive trees punch upwards through the scrub, dense spiky irregular branches laden with much smaller fruits than their domesticated cousins. A hidden Blackcap ticks away at me from deep within thick feral branches and, as I approach a large clump of these wild, ragged trees, I hear the distinctive sharp click of warning telling me that a Hawfinch is present. Wild Olives are great places to find these large, robust, but often shy finches. They feed hidden within the maze of branches, breaking open the fruit's stone-hard kernels with an audible crack using their outsized, powerful bills to good effect, exerting a force that would shatter our teeth if we tried it. I search for a view of this beautiful bird, trying to glimpse a movement amongst the thick foliage, but before I can find it amongst the grey green leaves, it is off, flying away from me on broad, boldly barred wings, the abrupt white end of the short tail catching my eye before it vanishes into another clump of trees below.

I start to descend deeper in to the valley itself, the smooth rolling terrain now replaced by a more angular, harder, uncompromising one, the stone path beneath my feet more polished, more worn than it was on the gentler slope. A young stag, a pricket in the terminology of deer watchers, crashes noisily down through the steep sea of green Cistus scrub to my left, dropping rapidly into a long, dry gully. It stands on the stony bottom and looks around, a confused mixture of testosterone-fuelled excitement and fear. He is no match for the mature stags roaring their claims to the groups of hinds in the surrounding countryside; he can't compete with their strength, but his hormones and the pheromones keep drawing him back to within their domains.

A majestic Golden Eagle soars up out of the valley, the bulging trailing edge of the wings, which terminate in their splay of finger-like primaries, distinctive as the bird breaks through the horizon and into the sky. A mottled mixture of dark browns and greys, capped by the signature golden nape, the bird rises quickly through the air until switching to a more active flight mode. Deep, slow deliberate wing beats interspersed with short glides lend the bird a majestic air as it heads off purposefully towards the dehesa. I watch it go, watching the intense raptor as it powers its way through the air.

The track I am following turns sharply to the west, entering the high-sided valley of the river, the walls of which now tower steeply upwards as well as dropping sharply down. It is at this point that the already steep-sided valley of the Salor tightens into a narrow gorge. In just a few paces the open landscape of Cistus scrub has been replaced by a more confined rocky one where the spiky, tangled wild Olives form clumps and establish a foothold amongst the otherwise dominant rock. Below me, the river is restricted to a series of narrow, deep pools encased in stone, their furious flow long cut off by the summer drought, but the potential of flow can be clearly seen in the scarred, gouged-out gorge. Polished rock sides, carved-out cauldrons and a multitude of smooth eroded shapes are testament to the mighty force this river has when in full flow.

It is in this perilous landscape that the old mine workings still stand, industrial relics of hewn stone, a towering wheel house, a collapsed dam and its rubble-filled leat, and a large rectangular stone platform, mind-bogglingly built on the steep side of the valley in what appears to be a gravity-defying manner. The original purpose of this construction is not apparent to me, but it serves as an excellent bird observation platform, allowing great views up and down the gorge and the wider valley – the perfect place for some vulture watching.

Vulture numbers would have been lower when the mine was in operation. Their numbers were suppressed by direct and indirect persecution, as well as by the lower numbers of livestock spread over the countryside, which reduced the availability of food, but in locations like this – wild, remote places that provided secure nesting sites – they would have been a very familiar sight to the miners that laboured here. What would these subterranean workers have made of these huge birds flying past them as they prepared to enter the claustrophobic shafts? Death and severe injury would have been occupational hazards to these workers; seeing birds associated with death would most probably have been an unwelcomed reminder of the potential hazards they faced. They may even have seen them as omens.

Human superstition has long associated the vulture with predicting death. The bird's appearance was believed to signify forthcoming disaster, but these birds are not auguries of impending doom; they are, instead, skilled readers of what is happening in the present, not in the future. The vultures were in this valley when the mine was operating because it provided secure nest sites and access to good foraging areas, much as it does today. They weren't there predicting disaster; they were there getting on with their lives. When animal carcasses are laid out for vultures at feeding stations, the birds have learnt to read cues in our behaviour as a sign that food will soon become available. The opening of the photographic hides, the movement of vehicles, the activities of humans on the ground, they can all be read and understood by these observant birds. Their behaviour in response to ours is then read and understood by other vultures in the visibility chains and, before long, the birds are already gathering ahead of the actual carcass being laid out. Like the fairground charlatans of the past, the birds can't see the future, but they can read the cues of the here and now and interpret the likely outcome.

It isn't long before I see the first vultures – four birds flying in close formation high above the valley. Instead of causing me to worry about my mortality, about the prospect of a calamitous accident, the sight of these four Griffon Vultures fills me with joy and awe. They are beautiful creatures, an example of evolutionary perfection, they are a keystone species in many of Europe's ecosystems, without them the natural world just doesn't function properly, and their presence is something to celebrate.

The four are flying in a diagonal formation, equally spaced for aeronautical efficiency, a sort of follow-my-leader where the followers benefit from residual lift created by the wings of the bird in front. They are too high to be coming back to the valley, flying in a south-westerly direction against a background of blue sky and cotton wool-like white clouds. I wonder to myself whether they are birds from the colony in the pines close to Portuguese border, heading back home after foraging on the plains; they are certainly heading in that rough direction. If so, they have about another fifty or so kilometres to cover. It won't take them long.

A vulture gliding serenely through the air can be doing so deceptively fast.

When you watch a vulture in the sky, watch its effortless flight as it glides serenely on wings that never seem to flap, it is easy to conclude that the birds are travelling relatively slowly. But the Griffon Vultures that have just flown past me, leaving me long behind already, are capable of travelling long distances at surprising speeds. Recently, a Griffon Vulture that had been caught and fitted with a GPS tracking system, was tracked travelling at nearly one hundred and twenty kilometres per hour, that's about seventy-five miles an hour – faster than the legal speed limit on Britain's motorways!

It is all about our perception of scale – a large vulture, high in the wide-open sky, doesn't look anywhere near as fast as a small bird flying in a cluttered, confined landscape. As I watch the Crag Martins below me, grey brown shadows flying across the rock faces, darting agilely after insects, their flight always busy, always active, their wings flapping at an improbably high rate, they seem ridiculously fast to me. But the reality is that they are probably only reaching speeds in the region of twenty-five miles an hour. Vultures are very fast birds, they need to be, the visibility chains they use to detect food may be tens of kilometres long and the vultures already down at the carcass are not going to wait for latecomers.

The not so fast but still dashing Crag Martins capture my attention for several more minutes, sweeping through the gorge, arcing across the rock faces, flashing the white mirrors in their tails as they bank sharply in acrobatic pursuit of small flying insects. A Blue Rock Thrush hops up onto the flat slate-topped parapet wall just a few metres along from me, a splash of vibrant colour in this landscape of dark stone and rock. It eyes me suspiciously for a few moments and then jumps off the wall, dropping straight down for several metres before opening his wings and flying across to a large rounded rocky promontory on the other side of the valley.

For some time, the roar of a stag has been growing louder and gradually getting closer. The sound rumbles off the rocks all around me and now he comes into my field of view.

The opposite side of the valley switches quickly from steep gorge to a more gentle tree- and scrub-covered slope, and it is here that he appears, walking along with a swagger, stopping occasionally to throw back his head and roar his importance for all to hear. His antlers are large and well balanced, and he uses them to unfairly attack a nearby Cistus bush that he has taken unknown umbrage with, thrashing his bony growths repeatedly through the straggly branches until they become adorned with broken-off sprays of leafy twigs. Satisfied with his assault on the local flora, he roars once more and begins to head up the slope into the dehesa beyond, the Cistus branches still dangling from his antlers, giving this mighty animal a somewhat comical aspect.

A far-off crack of a rifle reverberates sharply through the air, the stag pauses at the sound of it, looks around briefly, but soon continues on his way, untroubled by the sound that has probably just brought death to one of his brethren. Deer stalking is a popular pursuit in this area and one that brings money and jobs to the locality; indeed, much of the dehesa around me is managed with it in mind. But along with the money and the jobs, it also brings with it a danger to the vultures – lead ammunition.

Lead poisoning is a significant and widespread threat to vultures in many parts of the world, but it is also an often overlooked one. Game hunters and deer stalkers may not remove the whole of the shot animal from the environment; they may take just the head or a haunch, leaving the rest of the carcass behind. This may even be done deliberately to benefit scavengers such as vultures, providing them with a meal. But it is potentially a meal laced with lead.

Lead ammunition breaks up as the bullet hits the animal, causing fragments of this highly toxic metal to spread throughout the carcass. When vultures arrive to feed on a deer carcass they don't delicately feed on the finest cuts, they rapidly consume all parts of it, ingesting any lead present as they do so. There is no safe level when it comes to the amount of lead in a bird's body, or ours to that matter. Low-level lead poisoning may not directly kill the bird, but it can affect how it controls its metabolic rate, leading to birds overheating or losing weight. It can affect breeding success, damaging the long-term prospects of breeding colonies, and alter the bird's behaviour and nervous system, making them potentially more prone to collisions with wind turbines and electric pylons. It can also lower their immune system, making them more vulnerable to bacterial infections that they would normally be able to fight off.

Lead is a silent killer, one that is hard to detect and is easily missed when assessing the cause of death. It is easy to see that a vulture found dead under a wind turbine could have been killed by a physical collision with the structure, but it isn't easy to see what may be the actual underlying cause of the collision in the first place. It is only recently that scientific research has enabled conservation organisations to highlight the dangers of lead ammunition in the environment and this has already led to positive action, with many areas of Europe banning or restricting its use in locations where vultures are present, particularly those areas where the Bearded Vulture has been so successfully reintroduced across the European Alps.

The California Condor is an iconic New World vulture; it is also, sadly, one of the rarest birds on the planet. In the 1980s, the wild population had fallen to just sixty-seven individuals. Extinction seemed likely, but thanks to an intensive conservation effort since then, the population has recovered and now numbers around the five hundred mark. However, until very recently the birds were still dying prematurely and research showed that lead poisoning was the number one mortality cause for these magnificent birds. The continued use of lead ammunition in the areas where these giant birds lived was impacting the chances of them ever fully recovering from their 1980's nadir. To prevent further poisoning, the state of California acted quickly and boldly, banning the use of lead ammunition for hunting purposes throughout the entire state in a move that will hopefully safeguard the continued recovery of this threatened species.

More Griffon Vultures start to come in to view, these birds are lower than the first four that flew by a few minutes previously and, as they begin to approach the Salor, they start to lose height, beginning their descent into the valley, banking around, angling their wings back and lowering their legs. A few of the birds pass fairly close to where I am standing and I can see that their crops are full; they have recently fed and are now returning to the ledges sated. In the free-for-all at a carcass, vultures eat as quickly as they can, using their long necks to reach deep within the animal's body to get at the choicest morsels, wolfing food down before it is eaten by another. Once their stomachs are full, they fill their crops too – something to digest later, away from the chaos of the feeding frenzy. Carrion feeders can't guarantee where or when their next meal will come from, and even when it does come, they might not be allowed the opportunity to get much from it, such is the competition around a carcass. Their crop gives them the opportunity to take more than they can immediately digest, meaning that they maximise the amount of food available to them when they get the chance to get it. Grab what you can, when you can – a vulture survival strategy.

An adult Griffon Vulture typically weighs around ten kilograms, but a bird loaded with food in its stomach and its crop, which can hold around a kilogram of food itself, weighs a lot more. The maximum weight ever recorded was for a Griffon that had been caught shortly after feeding on a carcass on the island of Sardinia, it weighed in at over fifteen kilograms. The birds coming in to land now may be well loaded, but they still land on the narrow ledges with their usual consummate ease and, after a few loud arguments about who goes where, the birds settle down to digest their food in silence.

More birds start to arrive, returning to the ledges, and amongst them are some of this year's young. Their fresh plumage still noticeable – nice, regular, smooth outlines to the trailing edge of their wings and tail. The lack of moult in the feathers are indicative of their age and, as they come right by me, close enough for me to hear the soughing of the breeze over their wings, the uniformly dark bill confirms their immaturity.

Immature in terms of age they may be, but these youngsters are no longer the clumsy flyers of June. Mastering the air currents generated by the narrow gorge, they too land on its narrow ledges without any difficulty. However, unlike the first birds to arrive, these youngsters land on the ledges on the edge of the colony, sub-prime property rather than a desirable address. There is a strict hierarchy in Griffon colonies and the young of the year, once they become independent, find themselves at the bottom of it.

In a month or so, many of these young birds will start to wander, travelling across the wider vulture landscape. Some will stay in the Iberian Peninsula, using their flight skills to explore its vastness and covering long distances in just a few days. Others will head down to the south coast, crossing the narrow strip of sea at Gibraltar and heading to Africa to spend the winter there, travelling as far down as Senegal on the western edge of the continent, or taking a more central route over the sands of the Sahara to Niger in the heart of the continent.

The adult birds, the ones on the best ledges in the gorge, are generally residents, their nomadic wandering days are behind them. They will still clock up the miles as they patrol their vast home ranges and travel hundreds of kilometres each day as they scour the landscape beneath them, but they will return to their roosting cliffs when the day draws to an end.

More vultures fly past in loose formation, too high to be returning to this stretch of the valley. As they pass over it, they draw looks from the ledges below. Vultures vulture watch even more than I do.

OCTOBER

The body of the stag doesn't take long to be discovered. The once mighty, majestic animal, exhausted and fatigued by the exertions of the rut and spavined by an antler slash across the thigh of its back leg, has succumbed to the inevitable. A Raven feeds around the open wound, using its heavy bill to cleave off morsels of meat, hurriedly rushing to wolf down a meal before the circling vultures overhead claim it for their own. There are several Griffon Vultures and two Black Vultures wheeling above the densely crowned Evergreen Oaks of the dehesa. They have been circling for several minutes now, wary of the cover provided by the trees and unable to see the ground around the carcass, their shadows forming dancing figures flitting between the trees as they try to get a look. A party of Azure-winged Magpies drop delicately into the surrounding oaks, one after another, moving carefully towards

Vultures circling over the dehesa, the presence of the trees makes them wary of landing immediately; instead, they circle for several minutes until they are satisfied that all is well.

the carcass. Like their familiar black and white cousins, they are happy to feed on carrion should they get the opportunity to do so.

A Blackbird alarm calls, metallic harshness in amongst the greens of the wooded grassland; the Azure-winged Magpies join in with their rasping call; and Spotless Starlings fly up from the grass abandoning the leatherjackets they have been probing for to seek sanctuary in the trees. A Short-toed Treecreeper, hitherto busy probing the gnarled bark of a twisted, contorted trunk with its curved, fine tweezer-like bill, pauses to watch what is unfolding. Some of the magpies leave the trees, their long tails undulating behind them as they fly towards the source of the consternation. A Red Fox, its nose attuned to opportunity, is trotting through the grass, weaving between the trunks and heading for the carcass. The magpies show their displeasure with the fox, flashing blue wings as they fly low over it, but the fox is not to be distracted by such frivolities. The Raven gives an angry unhappy cronk and takes to the wing, crop bulging, as the fox approaches closer. The Treecreeper, unconcerned by the ground-dwelling predator, resumes its probing in its vertical world.

The fox carefully inspects the carcass, sniffing around the bulk lying in the grass until it gets to the wound on the rear thigh. The Raven has enlarged the hole in the hide, creating a chance for the fox to get easy access to the flesh inside, and it wastes no time. But it is out of luck. The Vultures have seen enough, whether it is the competition of the fox or whether they have satisfied themselves that their wary reticence is unjustified, they start to descend, the black shadows get bigger, congregating on the stricken deer. One bird lands a few metres from the scavenging carnivore, who turns to bare its teeth in a vicious snarl at the vulture. Dwarfing the fox, the Griffon half opens its wings in response, arching them in to a forward posture, lowering its head and extending its neck towards the animal, hissing its threat towards the mammalian competitor. The vulture hops forward on its massive feet, others landing around it. The fox can't compete and it snatches one last bite at the carcass before it's off, bounding across the grass as more vultures rain in.

The first Griffon gets to the wound, placing one of its oversized clawed feet onto the leg of the dead animal. It grabs at the damaged hide with its large bill, gripping it securely. The name 'vulture' comes from the Latin word *vulturus* meaning tearer. They are well named. Anchored by its feet, the Griffon uses its powerful neck muscles to rip open the damaged hide, tearing an ugly flap off with ease and exposing the muscle beneath. Just before the melee commences, it uses the sharp edges of its bill to slice off a chunk of flesh. The bird's tongue, covered in backward-pointing spines, grips the slippery morsel easily and it is quickly gulped down.

The first Black Vulture lands and hops directly towards where the carcass is obscured by the increasing mass of Griffons. Brown wings flap open as birds jump and hop into one another, jostling others out of the way, before they themselves are forced to yield. The second Black Vulture lands and immediately jumps towards the first Black, which immediately backtracks away from the carcass and the evidently high-ranking newcomer. The second bird, with wings drooped forward holds the pose momentarily, staring hard at the first, putting it firmly in its place, before it turns and wades into the fray, the Griffons parting for it without dissension.

Being close to vultures feeding is not necessarily a pleasant experience for the faint hearted – tempers flare between the birds and a whole host of strange hissing and gurgling noises emanate from them as they battle for the choicest pieces. Torn flesh and ripped viscera can be seen fleetingly between the chaos of the birds, the snap and crack of bones under the assault is audible and blood-covered heads and necks turn to look in your direction. Pretty it isn't; effective it is. The carcass of the deer is reduced to matted hair and bone in minutes.

The sated Griffons walk, hop, jump and waddle in their ungainly manner away from the remains of the stag, moving up the incline to an area where the trees are thinner in distribution. Here they feel more secure in their digestion, able to see more of the immediate area around them, as well as being able to use the slope below as a take-off aid if necessary. Being burdened with a full cargo of food makes take-off more laborious, a downhill runway will ease the effort required. Above them, more vultures circle the scene, lured in by the activity, but they're too late to reap the rewards of their effort, and they begin to gain height and slowly disperse across the sky.

For many months of the year, vultures dominate the skies of the region, dominating it not only by their sheer size, but also in quantity, simply outnumbering all other large birds in the air. This dominance by number is about to end; October sees a new arrival in the skies over this vulture landscape – Common Cranes.

They begin to arrive in dribs and drabs, small family groups heralding their arrival with trumpeting calls ringing across the sky. As the numbers build up, these small groups

After feeding, vultures will often walk up small inclines to give themselves a downhill runway, making it easier for them to take off quickly if they are disturbed.

A small ribbon of Common Crane making its way across the sky.

begin to become longer irregular lines in the sky as more and more birds arrive in their hundreds, then their thousands and then their tens of thousands. The undulating lines of cranes look ribbon-like as they make their way across the clouds. Just as swallows signify the coming of spring, the ribbons of cranes in October portend the arrival of winter.

Long-legged and long-necked, these elegant arrivals from the north are drawn to the region by the abundance of ripening acorns in the dehesa, as well as to the wetland refuges created by the irrigated rice fields. A significant proportion of Europe's breeding cranes come to Extremadura to overwinter, with numbers peaking over one hundred thousand in most years. They dominate the skies in the early morning and again at dusk when they return to their chosen roost sites, but during the day they are busy feeding, replenishing themselves after their long journey and, as the winter progresses, building up their reserves ahead of their trek back northwards.

With the Cranes come more birds from the north. Red Kites and Common Buzzards arrive, bolstering the numbers of the two species in the region. Lapwings and Golden Plovers form large loose-scattered flocks across the plains and become jumpy at the sight of another winterer – the Hen Harrier as it quarters the vast openness of grass, mirroring the actions of the now-gone, summering Montagu's.

Vultures are also moving. Most of the Egyptian Vultures will have embarked on their journey south by the middle of the month, although some do now stay all year around. These black and white vultures travel across the Straits of Gibraltar and down along the western edge of Africa to their wintering grounds in Mauritania and Mali. The peak time for Griffon Vultures to cross the Straits is also the middle of this month when youngsters and non-breeders embark on their winter peregrinations south. But the Black Vulture doesn't follow the example of the other two species; it is largely a sedentary bird, especially the adults. They may roam large distances during the day in their search for food, but they stay within their core areas and don't generally display the same desire to travel as the other two species do.

However, there are exceptions to the rule. Most years individual Black Vultures are reported near to the Straits and a few do indeed cross, but the short journey between continents is only fourteen kilometres and it is likely that they are just following the air currents rather than actually migrating. Black Vultures regularly fly sixty or seventy kilometres a day foraging, and so a day trip to Africa and back is well within their capabilities. However, there is plenty of evidence to show that some of the youngsters will travel much further – a chick ringed in a nest in the province of Madrid was found six months later in Senegal, over three thousand kilometres away. Another bird, again rung as a youngster, this time in the vulture landscape of Extremadura, was next seen in Mali two months later, having undertaken a three thousand kilometre plus trip. Black Vultures certainly have the ability to make long distance movements, just as young Griffons do, but generally they are content to stay within their breeding area throughout the year.

Ravens are tumbling in the sky, folding their wings in and performing rolling somersaults before opening out their long wings again and giving as joyful a cronk as a Raven can muster. Below them the Tajo river stagnates its way through the chain of dams that impede its path as it heads towards the far-off Atlantic. The Raven's playful acrobatics soon take them across the valley. Several Griffon Vultures cross it too, but in a somewhat less frivolous manner than the large corvids.

Lower down, in the broad V of the valley, a party of Azure-winged Magpies flash blue as they fly low up the steep terraced slopes, pitching into a group of well-tended Olives and decorating the silvery grey leaves of the neatly pruned trees with their soft azure hues. With their blue wings and tail, their buffish, brown-pink bodies, pale throat and matt black cap, the Azure-winged Magpie is a very beautiful bird. The highly social corvids below me are foraging up the slope, using the Olives and other trees as both cover and vantage points, dropping down from them to the grasses below to feed on whatever catches their dark eyes. From my own vantage point, I can watch them with ease. I am standing at the point where the old track crosses out of the terraced valley and into the stone-walled graz-

A couple of Black Vultures taking to the air out on the plains of the vulture landscape.

The Azure-winged Magpie is a highly social member of the Corvid family and can often be seen flashing its lovely blue as it flies through the dehesa.

ing fields, the point where the steep terrain of the river-cut geology meets the smoother land of the plateau above.

It is a panoramic viewpoint, named the balcony of the world, and the old track leading to it now is waymarked and upgraded to encourage people to use it. But I am the only one here and looking back through the valley below me, looking at the track as it first zigzags and then follows a contour, I can see that I will not be joined by anybody any time soon. I look east up the dark river at the triumphal Roman bridge as it links the two cleaved sides of the Extremaduran countryside, the impressive architectural glory of this near two-thousand-year-old structure somewhat dimmed by the huge wall of concrete just beyond it. Hydroelectric dams are not known for their aesthetics.

From where I am standing, stone walls radiate out in all directions, partitioning the rough grassy terrain into a myriad of small fields. A loose group of Corn Buntings are moving through some of the fields behind me, the dry click of their contact call coming from them as they go, sometimes pausing to feed amongst the grasses, other times stopping on the carefully built walls. Another bunting pops up, pitching on to the lichen-dominated stone that caps the wall in front of me, showing me the typical streaky back of the family. But this one is slightly smaller and daintier than the Cornies and, as it hops over the stones, it turns to the side to reveal that it has a delicately striped head with dark lines contrasting against the pale-yellow background colour – a female Cirl Bunting, an often unnoticed, but common, member of the avian community here. She sits in all her glory for a few seconds before dropping down to the field on the other side of the wall to continue looking for grass seeds.

Above the buntings, and above me, three Griffon Vultures are meandering their way along the moving rivers of the sky, irregular trailing edges of their wings showing their moult patterns clearly. Three individuals in three different places following three different routes, but all three are very aware of what the other two are doing. Watching them carefully you can see them looking at one another all the time, turning their heads when needing to keep them in view. The angled mass of concrete that is the dam may not be the most aesthetic structure in the landscape, but it does create huge uplift. One of the vultures enters this column of concrete-powered rising air, soaring with the primaries splayed out, the bird gains height with ease. One of the other vultures changes their direction of flight slightly, watching the first, circling, climbing bird.

An adult Griffon Vulture in flight showing the irregular trailing edge due to moult and the pale bill which signifies its maturity.

Vultures are always observing one another, continuously keeping tabs on what the others are doing; nothing escapes them. It is what makes them efficient scavengers, but it also makes them efficient flyers. By watching how others are flying, what route they are following in the sky, what lifts they are taking, what turbulence they are encountering, the watchers can plot their own routes. The first bird stays in the thermal only briefly, slipping out of it and into a fast glide, visibly descending as it heads towards the direction of the quarry. The dam's thermal was used to gain enough height so that the bird could drop back to the roost site without expending energy. The watching second bird alters its course again, losing interest in what the first is doing, now that it understands the motives for the bird's movements.

From my vantage point I get a good snapshot of the visibility chains formed by the vultures. Using my binoculars, I can see several of them spread out across the landscape, each one busy observing others. Some of the birds are very high, beyond the range of my eye, but just visible through the magnified glasses. These are neck-breaking altitudes for observers like me on the ground, and I rest my craned neck by focusing on the easier to view antics of the Corn Buntings once more. Another small brown bird is sitting on a rock on the steep sloping terrain of the valley side. It is a lark with a distinct crest, but it isn't a Crested Lark, it is the very similar Thekla Lark, a bird that causes much confusion for visiting bird watchers. In its fresh autumn plumage, the Thekla below me is a clearer-marked bird than its close relation, with clearer markings on the bird's chest and face compared to the more ubiquitous Crested. The Thekla's crest is neat and compact, much more fan-like than the rather spiky, longer crest of the Crested. It is this, coupled with the smaller bill, that is key to identifying which of the larks you are looking at.

A Black Redstart female jumps up onto one of the walls. More subtle in plumage than the showy male, her red undertail is nonetheless noticeable as she flicks it in nervous agitation at discovering my presence close to where she was foraging for insects. She hops off the wall again, dropping down into the field beyond the wall and out of sight. A group of Meadow Pipits fly in and land in the field in front of me, happy, it would seem, to feed in my presence even if the redstart isn't. As I watch these new arrivals busily feeding in front of me, my ears pick up on the faint, far-off call of cranes.

A bugle call announcing their return, an evocative call that has been missing from the skies of the vulture landscape since the beginning of March when the last of these graceful travellers headed back north to breed. It is a welcome sound and one that has me immediately scanning for a sight of its makers. The far-carrying call is distant and hard to locate, drifting to my ears rather than coming to them from any specific direction. Eventually I see them – a straggly ribbon of six birds, presumably heading for the traditional roost site a few miles east from where I am watching them.

I decide to head there myself to welcome the birds back. Walking briskly along the shortest path back to the town, skirting the old Moorish walls with their tumbling Prickly Pear cactus growing out of the large cracks, I pause momentarily to watch a male Black Wheatear flash its white rump at me as it flies up to the top of the Arabic wall. I drive through the narrow streets of the old town and out onto the wide straight road that heads east, turning onto the network of tracks that lead to a large area of dehesa and grazing fields. The area doesn't look any different to me than any others found in the locality, but the cranes obviously see it as being different because every year over a thousand of them use it as their roost, filling the skies and the dehesa with their trumpet chorus.

I spot birds straight away – two adults and their youngster, standing suspiciously in a field strewn with granite protrusions on the edge of the dehesa. All three appear nervous, warily striding about the grassy field, unsure of what to do next. I stop the car as soon as I see them, remaining several hundred metres away from them. These birds will have just arrived and the last thing they need is to be forced back into flight again by my over-eagerness to see them. The adult birds, with their long black and white necks, gradually relax and begin to feed, probing the ground beneath them. The youngster, who lacks the neck and head markings of the adults, keeps close to them, but seems unable to comprehend what is happening. This bird would have hatched from its egg, probably in one of the boreal forest bogs of Scandinavia during June, and now, only a few months later, it has just completed an epic migration and finds itself in an unknown environment. The youngster should have a sibling with it – Common Cranes have two chicks as a rule – but there is only one present now, the other may have perished in the nest or it could have died during the migration. Flying thousands of miles within a few weeks of fledging takes a toll.

As I watch them from within the car, another family of cranes lands in the field, two adults again, but this time with two youngsters in tow. The landing adults announce their arrival with loud sonorous calls, a delightful sound that brings a smile to my face. There are a few more birds in the skies above now, the cranes are gathering and the sound of approaching winter is all around. Conscious of not disturbing the weary travellers, I leave them to arrive in peace and I back up the track before taking another one that leads me out to a small village, dominated as always by the huge church in its midst. But there is another building that catches the eye here. A single storey community building that would be nondescript were it not for its decoration – a fantastic mural of cranes, a migrating flock, necks outstretched, flying across the colourful wall. Cranes are very much part of the community.

An early morning start sees me driving north out of the village. It is a chilly morning with the sun only beginning to show itself as a faint glow on the eastern horizon as I start my descent into the Salor valley, a thick mist hanging stubbornly in it, obscuring the view and coating the car in wetness. The mist dissipates once I climb back out of the valley and onto the plains, but streams of it persist in places, clinging to the landscape, waiting for the sun to rise and evaporate them away. At the top of the first hill I go past, I see two dark figures hunched over. Black Vultures in damp black overcoats. I slow the car down and, as I do so, two heads pop up out of the black overcoats to observe what I am doing. A car travelling across the plains is normal, but a car slowing down is not. The vultures know this and cautiously observe what I am doing.

I pull over in a gateway on the opposite side of the road from where the vultures are watching me. Their plumage is glistening as the light rapidly improves with the approaching dawn, the beads of moisture lending their coat a glossy black appearance. Their pale bald head pattern that is clearly visible as they look at me watching them indicates that they are full adults, despite the apparent blackness of their plumage. The sun breaks the horizon and bathes the two birds in its warmth. They have evidently overnighted out here on the plain and that can only mean one thing – the presence of food close by.

Black Vultures will generally leave a feeding site to return to their roost before sunset. But if they come across a food source late in the day, they will sometimes opt to sit out the night by it rather than risk flying back to the roost in low visibility. By doing this they are then able to continue feeding at first light the following morning. They won't do this if they don't feel secure in the location, but on a small hill in the open landscape of the plain they evidently felt safe enough, no doubt aided by the clear night that would have offered them some limited visibility.

With the sun now up, the birds waste little time looking at me ensconced in my car as I use it as a hide to watch these two giants of the bird world. They shake themselves down, much like a falcon about to take off, and water droplets spray off them in all directions. With the moisture gone, their plumage turns from the dark black of before to a very dark brown, confirming their adult status. Dewatered, they waddle one after another with their ungainly gait down the slope, occasionally pausing to look around them and at me. They don't walk far and soon stop, having another quick look around before the first bird lowers its head and begins to feed on a carcass that is obscured from my vision by the lay of the land.

Unlike Griffon Vultures, Blacks are fussy about who they will share their meals with. They will ignore Griffons feeding at a carcass and because they are much more dominant than their smaller relatives, they can easily bully them out of the way if they need to. Griffons know this and subserviently give their bigger relatives all the space they wish. But Black Vultures don't like other Black Vultures feeding close to them, and there is much posturing and full-on fighting if two of these gargantuan vultures try to share food at the same time. If you see Black Vultures at a carcass, one bird will feed whilst the others bide their time, usually pacing around in a frustrated manner, and only when the first has sated itself does the next bird enter the fray. The fact that these two are now feeding right next to each other tells me that these two birds are a pair. Reaching maturity at five or six years old, the Black Vulture forms a monogamous lifelong pairing with its mate. The bond between them is very strong and they will often be seen together throughout the year. This bond lasts a long time, and with wild Black Vultures living in to their thirties, this pair could be together for over twenty-five years.

Using its strong feet as a clamp, the first bird lowers its bald head and pulls hard on the flesh of the carcass with its massive bill, tearing it free with ease. The bird swallows it down with a gulp and then raises its neck fully upright to have a good look around whilst the second bird dips its head and helps itself. A small piece of dirty white wool wafts in the air by the two birds; the unseen food is evidently a sheep carcass. They would have started to feed on it last night and probably continued to feed for a while after the sun had set. Now, with the new day dawned, they are free to consume the rest of their meal long before it is discovered by others. I look at my watch and realise that I am now a long way behind schedule. I restart the engine, causing both birds to stand and stare at me again. I move off, driving along the road and leave them to the feast they waited all night for. Running late in this vulture landscape can be an all too regular occurrence.

NOVEMBER

The lone Griffon Vulture laboriously flaps its large wings beneath the tenebrous sky, ever-increasing shades of heavy grey foretelling an imminent, prolonged soaking. The vulture is in a hurry, it will not want to fly in the rain – wet heavy feathers and gusty winds do not make for efficient flying conditions. Vultures dislike the rain. It will want to get back to its roosting ledge, back to the colony, to sit out the impending downpour. If it can't make it back before the rain, it will have to settle for an alternative rock outcrop, perhaps even a pylon or a tree, any port in a storm will do. To see a Griffon Vulture on a ledge in the rain, huddled there with droplets of water cascading off its plumage, is to see the avian embodiment of misery.

The rain comes, but not the big heavy drought-breaking thunderous drops of September; just a steady, continuous rain, soaking everywhere and everything, permeating the landscape, saturating deep down within it, wetting long-dry buried soils. Water flows in rivulets, meeting other rivulets and bringing to life forgotten streams and pools. Ponds fill; they overflow. The rivers swell and their waters move with force once again. The downpour continues, the noise of the rivers increases, the waters roar crashing over rocks and washing away the debris of fallen branches, smashing them against the boulders. The rivers live again, and suddenly they are wild, exuberant masses of angry white water.

For two days the steady precipitation falls without abatement, for two days the skies are empty of vultures, grounded by the unceasing rain, a forced exile from the sky. Finally, a dry morning dawns and everywhere smells wet, fresh, renewed. The air is cold and clear, the dawn sky pale, ribbons of cranes, scrawled lines across the sky, leaving their roosts and heading to feed in this new wet, puddle-strewn landscape.

The clatter of the surging river reverberates around the walls of the Salor valley, and close to the water the noise is all-encompassing, deafening, unnerving in its potency. I clamber up the slippery hillside, away from the tumult below, until I reach the spot from where I can view the ledges, and then I see them, the vultures of the Salor. Some are on the roosting ledges, motionless, waiting for the air to signal the moment they can step off once again and reclaim their place in the sky, but others are more proactive, clambering ungainly up the valley sides, positioning themselves on pinnacles and small protrusions of rock, giving themselves space. They need the space for what they are doing, the space to dry their flight feathers, the space to unfurl their prodigious wings and opening them to the fullest extent, stretching them out cormorant style to dry in the breeze. Seeing them like this, seeing them grounded with wings outstretched, emphasises the sheer magnitude of the bird.

A Griffon Vulture hanging its wings out to dry following heavy rain.

Around me in the wet scrub, numerous wintering Blackbirds busy themselves flicking over the damp leaf litter with quick jabbing movements of their bills, cocking their heads to the side to detect any movement and then pouncing rapidly on to its source. Another wintering traveller from the north, a Robin, red breast proudly on show, watches carefully, waiting its chance to profit. Blackbirds and Robins, a scene from a suburban British garden, but instead of the clothes drying in the wind, it is the wings of the vultures that have been hung out to dry.

The driving force of the river, smashing and crashing through the steep cleaved rock creates a forceful turbulence of air, swirling rivers of wild wind driven by swirling wild waters. Two dark Ravens ride this unpredictable rollercoaster of currents, revelling in it, folding wings and tumbling, barrelling through it, before opening their flight feathers to rise vertically, momentarily hanging motionless, before once again letting the blast take them onwards, their gleeful calls almost lost in the elemental roar of the water below.

The vultures watch, trying to read the jumble of air currents streaming through the valley, one bird folds up its extended wings, rouses itself with a vigorous shake and then jumps upwards off the rock, its wings unfurl once more and instantly catch the wind, whisking it upwards. Deep, powerful wing beats restore control and suddenly the vulture is majestic again, wings held out, angled slightly upwards, soaring on the updraft, tight circles of flight, broadening out with altitude, it breaks free of the turbulent air below. Others follow, some stay low initially, driven at speed down the valley before they bank into the current and rapidly rise, the rocky ledges start to empty in quick succession, one after another the vultures shed their rain enforced shackles and regain their aerial realm.

Within minutes they are spreading out over the surrounding countryside, some heading south over the dehesa, others north over the plains, establishing the visibility chains once again. Two days without food is easily bearable for these birds that can fast for up to two weeks, but they will still be hungry and eager to find the next meal.

The fields have responded to the soaking, the grass grows again, a rapid lush growth and from this verdant carpet, a mass of Meadow Pipits suddenly rises as one. These birds have travelled from the wintery north and have brought with them an unwanted hanger on – a female Sparrowhawk, an immature bird that has followed her livelihood south across the continent. She powers purposefully through the air and into the rising mass of smaller birds. The pipits scatter, alarm calls jarring and a blur of action. Suddenly it is all over, a few tiny, soft downy feathers fall slowly to the earth, the hawk flies onward, a small brown shape grasped tightly in her talons. The pipits return to the field. A Hoopoe, alert on a fence post, flicks its fan-like crest up for a moment as if acknowledging the drama that has just unfolded.

Many birds, including vultures, rouse themselves before taking to the air by shaking their flight feathers.

I am about three kilometres outside the village, walking along a track that gently rises up from the narrow streets and their white-washed houses. The stone-walled open fields, in which I have just been watching the pipits and their predator, fall behind me and give way to dehesa. The small, tough spiky leaves of the oaks still glisten with moisture in the weak sunshine, and Azure-winged Magpies drop casually down from the branches, flashing their delicate blue as they land in the mass of grasses below, hopping and jumping in and out of view as they seek out their insect food. The track crunches audibly beneath my feet as I walk. The rain has brought substance to the fine particles of grit and sand that make up its surface, the soft puffs of dust generated by my steps in the summer along this same stretch are but a memory.

There is a distinct coolness to the day, the sun still has warmth, the temperature is pleasant, the sky is blue but it has that cold clear look to it that signifies winter has arrived, and when the sun dips below the western hills in a few hours' time, the temperature is going to drop with it. A Red Kite, deeply forked tail twisting, flies slowly over the damp landscape. I look at its beauty through my binoculars, at its vibrant-coloured rudder of a tail, its angled back wings and its pale head. I notice that its crop is bulging with food; it will have struggled to have found feeding opportunities these last two, rain filled days, but it has evidently made up for it now that the rain has abated once again.

I arrive at the old metal gates that I have been slowly heading for since I left the village. On the other side of the gates, the oaks of the dehesa are more ramshackle in appearance compared to the trees I have just walked past, and the grazing underneath them is not all grass, but a mixture of Cistus scrub, twiggy lavender and bare stony patches. I pull hard on the large rusty bolt that reluctantly yields to my wishes, sliding back with a harsh grating noise and releasing the gate. Much of the dehesa you see in this vulture landscape provides an excellent habitat, but it is a habitat that is still very much managed for the grazing of sheep and cattle. This quiet, almost forgotten patch isn't. It has its stock fencing around its perimeter, but it has been left to go, quite literally, to seed. As a result, it abounds with life.

The thin soil at times fails to cover the rocky substrate beneath and the grey stone ridges poking through create angular shapes across the surface. Only where the soil has any real depth do you find grasses. In the shallower soils, the Cistus dominates, whilst on the very thin soils, patches of lavender grow, small carpets creating an almost Hardy-like heath. The vibrant purple of the flowers are just spring and summer memories, but as I walk through these brittle plants, their strong, clean, aromatic scent rises from under my feet to greet me. A Woodlark, no longer the cautious bird of the breeding season, watches me pass by before it walks off through the maze of lavender twigs. A small group of Linnets rise in front of me, twittering as they do so. They don't go far, wheeling round to the left before dropping down to an area where the grasses meet the barer soils to resume their continual search for small seeds.

I make my way to the old stock pond hewn out of the hard, stony ground by hand many years ago. A stone wall around two sides of it has become a lichen-clad tumbledown vestige of what it must have looked like when first built, but it provides me with the perfect place

The jangly song of the Corn Bunting can be heard throughout the vulture landscape.

to sit down and take in all that is happening around me. The heads of several frogs poke up through the surface of the water, watching me suspiciously as I settle down. Further along the crumbled wall, a Thekla Lark is busy preening itself, whilst in an oak on the other side of the pond a Corn Bunting tumbles out its song before flying away from me. I don't see where it goes, but it announces its arrival with another short burst of its signature jangly melody.

A male Blackbird, that delightful contrast of light-consuming darkness and radiant yellow bill, clucks nervously away at my presence before unashamedly dissolving into full panic mode, flying away in a loud, sharp crescendo of alarm. Others ignore the scaremongering. Two Rock Sparrows with their boldly streaked heads land just a few metres away from me; they know I am here, they both give me a quick look, but they don't share the neurosis of the Blackbird and are soon drinking from the pond's edge.

This old stock pond is a great place to watch wildlife in close proximity, but it also allows me to see much further afield, offering an unspoilt panorama of the land that falls away from where I am sitting on my lichen-covered granite seat. It is from this spot that I really get to see the vulture landscape as it unfurls in front of me as far as my eyes can see. The gentle green folds of the immediate landscape descend for several kilometres to the harder, steeper undulations of the Salor valley, before rising onto the plains and continuing northwards until the hills begin again in the far distance. The clear sky enables me to see for many, many miles. I can see the mountains of Portugal. I can see that the recent rains have fallen as snow on the tops of the Sierra de Estrella, the highest part of Spain's western neighbour; another reminder that winter is here. My viewpoint is the perfect place to look out over the landscape and indulge in some vulture gazing.

There are birds over the Salor valley, probably five or six kilometres from where I am sitting. Even at this distance I can tell they are Griffon Vultures – their wings held in their characteristic shallow V. They are quite low down, but as I look, I spot others higher up above them. I scan across the landscape, seeing more individual vultures scattered about it as I do so. Further away from me still, I see a lot of vultures, gathering together in a circling stack; a kettle is forming. They appear to be over the plains. This is not a gathering of birds taking advantage of a rising current of air; this is a gathering of birds over potential food. My vantage point is too far away to see any detail – they are just distant birds circling – but it does give me the perfect opportunity to watch how the news of the potential food travels through the visibility chains.

The birds that I first saw are no longer randomly scattered individuals – they have become constituent parts of the aerial network and are all heading in the direction of the gathering kettle. The birds in the Salor valley have seen this network, seen this purposeful switch in behaviour. They have picked up on the newsfeed and are now tuning themselves in. The vultures that were high above the valley are already heading off and those lower down are changing their flight pattern, tightening their soaring circles, rising faster to escape the confines of the valley, eager to follow the birds that were above them.

How vultures find their food has fascinated naturalists for centuries; indeed, it has provoked fierce debate amongst many. Eminent luminaries such as Darwin and Audubon taxed their minds and argued via numerous scientific papers, letters and experiments on how these large birds found the dead. Many asserted it was by smell, but others argued it was by sight alone. The answer to this debate lies in where you are coming from. There are twenty-three species of vulture in the world, which fall broadly into two groups: the Old World vultures of Europe, Africa and Asia, and the New World vultures of the Americas.

These two groups are not actually closely related; indeed, they are very different from each other in many aspects, but, in a process known as convergent evolution, they have both evolved the basic vulture formula of being big, broad-winged birds that feed on carrion. The Old World vultures, such as those spread out across the sky before me, find their food by sight alone; the afore-mentioned visibility chains proving to be a very effective and efficient way of doing so. Most raptors don't have a sense of smell or at least, if they do, it is poorly developed, but some of the New World vultures do have a sense of smell, and in at least three of the species it is well developed indeed.

The Turkey Vulture, the Lesser Yellow-headed Vulture and the Greater Yellow-headed Vulture are all able to find carcasses by their sense of smell. Unlike the vast majority of birds, these three carrion feeders have well-developed olfactory receptors in their brains, enabling them to detect a chemical substance called ethyl mercaptan. This gaseous chemical is strong and has an unpleasant smell – even we humans can detect it. It is the characteristic aroma of dead bodies, and these three vultures of the Americas can detect small traces of it from up to a mile away.

So good are they at detecting it, that we have long exploited their sense of smell to help us find gas leaks. In the 1930s, engineers working on the above-ground gas pipelines in California noticed that Turkey Vultures would gather around pipes that were leaking – they were drawn to these sites due to the small amounts of ethyl mercaptan present in the gas. Whilst the vultures were no doubt confused and disappointed by the resulting lack of carcass, the engineers realised that by adding more of this chemical to the gas in the pipes, thereby making any future leak more attractive to the birds, it would enable them to be able to detect leaks in their pipeline far more quickly. Instead of expensive monitoring and tests, the engineers could indulge in some vulture watching instead.

Sight still plays a part for these vultures of the Americas of course. The smell may be what first catches their attention, first draws them in, but they use their vision to find its source and visibility chains play their part here too. Other species of the New World vultures, birds such as the King Vulture, are unable to detect death by smell, but they can watch what the smaller, odour-enabled birds are doing and they can read their behaviour in the same way that the Old World Griffon and Black Vultures can read the behaviour of Ravens and Black Kites. If a Lesser Yellow-headed Vulture starts to look as if it has detected food, then a King Vulture will switch course to follow it and investigate. Having a much larger species follow you to a carcass may at first seem like a disadvantage; the bigger bird will inevitably dominate the feeding opportunity, but the King Vulture is a powerful bird with an equally powerful bill and it can slice into the tough hides of animals, opening the carcass up far better than the smaller billed Yellow-headed who may otherwise struggle to do so. They may have to wait their turn, but once the King has fed, the smaller vultures can readily access food that would have been otherwise unavailable to them.

The visibility chains of the vultures in front of me have once again rapidly spread the news far and wide. A carcass has been found; the message broadcast to all. There are now many birds gathered in the kettle and, as I watch, they begin to drop downwards, individual birds, lowering their legs and dropping sharply towards the ground, disappearing from my vision as they do so, one after another. I look further afield and can see many more vultures dotted across all points of the compass converging hurriedly towards the site, high above me a Griffon Vulture passes overhead, gliding on outstretched wings in the direction of where the birds are now dropping in increasingly large numbers. A second Griffon goes over and then a Black Vulture follows. I watch the latter two birds in my binoculars as they rapidly move away from me. No matter how often I watch these birds, their ability to move quickly across the sky without seemingly any effort simply amazes me. In just a couple of minutes, they are over the Salor valley and into the turbulent air generated by the raging river below. Each bird turns into the valley, one after the other and following the same path. They first turn westwards, spiralling around in tight circles to gain height with alacrity, before emerging on the other side of the valley, high enough to continue their long gliding descent to where, hopefully, some food may remain.

The word kettle has long been used to describe a mass of vultures circling closely in the sky. The origins of the term are unclear, with some stating that the large swirling mass of birds is similar in appearance to the water moving in a boiling cauldron. Whatever the origin of the term, the kettle that I am watching in the distance soon begins to quickly fall apart; its constituents dropping rapidly to the ground, leaving only new arrivals to circle in it briefly, before they too head downwards.

After a few minutes, the behaviour of the birds still arriving begins to change. Instead of dropping straight down to join the undoubted melee taking place below, they now start to circle over the site, forming broad rings in the sky, a much looser looking kettle than before. The feeding must be coming to an end and the potential of food diminishing – the birds above have to assess their options. As with everything a vulture does, these options are governed by the economics of efficiency. Dropping down to the remains of a carcass doesn't cost much in terms of energy, but taking off again, getting their bulk airborne from the flat ground, does. The behaviour of the birds in the air, now flying in increasingly larger circles suggests that they have decided there is no longer any gain in them landing.

One of the circling birds breaks out of the broad kettle and heads eastwards. Initially I don't pay it any attention until I notice a second and then a third bird do the same. I look in the direction they are heading and much further to the east I see a small mass of vultures circling tightly. They are difficult for me to see at this distance, especially against a background of dehesa-clad hills, but the newly arriving vultures have seen them and are now changing course to join them. Perhaps their journey hasn't been wasted after all.

I spend an hour just vulture gazing, my mind lost in the blue sky in front of me. Occasionally I switch to a bit of vulture watching when a bit of behaviour catches my eye, but mostly I just sit and gaze, relaxing in the afternoon, emptying my mind and forgetting time. Vulture gazing has become an important part of my life. I never deliberately intended to become a vulture gazer; it just happened. There is something very relaxing about watching these massive birds drift through the sky with complete ease. It is therapeutic and enjoyable at the same time. Nature is good for us, and finding time to switch off and enjoy it is important. The unstructured world of vulture gazing is my natural therapy in this modern, busy world.

A shadow of a tree recalls me to reality as it begins to creep over where I am sitting. The temperature difference between the light and the shade is very noticeable; it is cold out of the sunlight. I stand up and have one last look out over the vista in front of me – most of what I can see is sky, an empty space to us land dwellers. But it isn't really empty. Vulture watching allows you to see that. You see that it is just as important a part of the landscape as the ground beneath it. It is the medium in which communications are carried by sight, by sound and, in some cases, smell. It is full of ever-changing highways, allowing the constant passage of all that is winged, from tiny flies to gigantic vulturine birds.

I walk back through the tired dehesa, crunching yet more aromatic stems beneath my feet. Goldfinches mixed with Linnets rise colourfully in front of me, and some Spanish Sparrows blur past in a small chattering flock whilst an Iberian Grey Shrike watches me intently with its white eyebrowed-topped beady eye. This dapper small predator is sitting on a dead branch sticking out of the small canopy of an Evergreen Oak. It is evidently happy that I am far enough away from it because it sits in the sun, unmoving; its feathers slightly puffed up against the lowering temperature. Tonight is set to be the first cold night since last winter, and it will come as a shock to much of the life here.

Iberian Grey Shrikes are small resident predators that often impale their meals on the barbs of barbed wire fences.

As I tramp back down the wide track that leads to the village, I notice the welcome return of some of my neighbours. These neighbours left the village in the arid heat of the summer and headed south, stopping at the irrigated rice fields in the south of the region perhaps, or even heading further south, popping across to Africa. Wherever they have been, the White Storks are now back. Two birds are flying over the terracotta roofs of the village, circling the prominent town hall and church where there are several huge stick nests that the storks use year after year. As I approach the flowing river on the edge of the village, I see another stork stalking through the margin of vegetation along the water's edge, making large purposeful strides, then stopping, watching intently, before moving forward again. The frog's nemesis has returned.

Just past the river, a fourth White Stork, presumably the mate of the one by the river, is standing on the edge of the nest that is seemingly precariously positioned on top of the pylon by the granary, bemusedly looking down to the deep bowl of sticks beneath its feet. I get a great view of this beautiful bird as I pass by – the clean white head, neck and body contrasting elegantly with the black of the wings, the red of the legs and bill adding a touch of warmth to its appearance. Shortly after I walk past, I hear the brilliant sound of bill clacking from behind me, and I turn to see both birds on the edge of the nest, their heads thrown right back across their backs as they clack their bills in what can only be described as a joyous celebration. A celebration of returning to their breeding site and a celebration of the strong pair bond that binds them to it.

Even though they won't be laying their eggs until the end of March or beginning of April, the nest will now be the focal point of their lives once again. They will immediately start renovating it, vigorously defend it against any other White Storks with usurpative thoughts, and will regularly spend time together on it, greeting one another with that delightful clacking sound. Winter may be about to properly arrive, but with the coming of sustained rain, the countryside is once again alive with life – and the White Storks have returned to be part of it.

The broad gravel track becomes a surfaced narrow street as I enter the village; the low granite stone walls that escorted me along the track replaced by towering white-washed house walls. A Spotless Starling, unseen on a chimney or aerial above me, whistles and chatters an anarchic welcome as I make my way through the maze. I turn into my street, breathing in the aromas of evening cooking and look up to see a Black Vulture flying high above it, heading in the direction of the wooded hills of the Sierra de San Pedro beyond. I wonder to myself if this is the bird I watched earlier, tailing the Griffon Vulture over the landscape in front of me, spiralling up on the air currents of the Salor valley before heading for the gathering of vultures circling out over the plains. Did it get to that carcass in time or did it divert to the other kettle that was forming many kilometres further east? I'll never know of course, but after a bit of vulture gazing and vulture watching you are always entitled to some vulture wondering.

White Storks are symbols of the region, as well as being the frog's nemesis.

DECEMBER

The motorway seems endless, as motorways often do, as it ploughs its way across the high meseta of northern Spain. Towns and cities come and go, names on signs, each one as they pass marking a step nearer to where I am returning. After the city of Salamanca, that ancient seat of learning, the terrain that the tarmac cuts through becomes more rugged and interesting. Those white-topped distant hills soon become the snowy landscape through which I am driving, and the huge imposing bulk of the Sierra de Gredos looms into view, their coat of white giving them a misleadingly gentle appearance.

The view as I near the end of the region of Castilla y Leon is picturesque, the tarmac curves smoothly like a dark grey ribbon through the snow-white hills and peaks. Above it is the clear blue winter sky, and in that sky a group of vultures are circling high. I am nearly there.

From a closed-in horizon of mountainous terrain, the world in front of me suddenly opens up and falls away. From my elevated position I can see for miles into the southern half of the country. Then I descend, dropping rapidly, as the motorway falls off the end of the ancient kingdom of Castille and lands several hundred metres below in Extremadura. The snow-clad hills are left behind and are now replaced with the familiar greens of the dehesa-clad ones – I am back within the vulture landscape.

Almost immediately, I see a Black Vulture gliding arrow-straight on its flat wings, travelling at speed and crossing the motorway far below it, ignorant of the irrelevant human traffic dropping into the southern half of Spain or climbing up to the north.

After a few more kilometres I stop at a service station for a much-needed caffeine hit. Griffon Vultures dot the sky and lower down a Red Kite is eagerly examining the tarmac expanse of the car and lorry parking. Atop the heavily branded services sign, a White Stork, standing on its unintentionally endorsed nest, greets its returning mate with a vigorous bout of bill clacking. Coffee taken, I rejoin the road and slowly climb upwards towards a small ridge, following the Ruta de Plata, the old Roman Silver Way that transported the metallic wealth of northern Iberia down to the Roman seat of power at Merida. Vultures are now a constant in the aerial skyscape as I crest the ridge and enter the Tajo watershed.

A few minutes later and I cross the river itself – a wide, deep valley of still, tamed water backed up by a dam many kilometres west. The valley may not be home to the once-rushing winter waters of the Tajo anymore, but it still generates lift and, as I look to my right, I see vultures using it, soaring on the uplift, fingered primaries splayed as they travel the sky's highways.

I come off the land-based fixed highway on which I have been travelling for hours, and move onto smaller routes that run parallel with the river just to the north of me, going through scruffy *Retama* scrub at first and then into and past the black-stemmed, currently leafless Almond trees planted in neat orchard rows flanking the road. Another orchard follows, but this time it has a more surreal feel, a landscape of lollipop trees and rolling grass-covered hills. Tall, straight trunks disappear into dense spherical canopies – green balls atop brown sticks. When a child draws a tree, they draw these ones. Stone Pines, the source of pesto-making pine nuts, dot the landscape around me, their distinctive lollipop shape characteristic of the species. We have been cultivating these trees for thousands of years, harvesting their highly nutritious seeds and creating these large orchards of lollipop trees.

An improbably big black shape breaks the rounded green top of one of the lollipops – a Black Vulture. It is watching over the orchard and surveying the landscape. The upright posture, fluffed up neck feathers and bald head combines to give the bird the monastic look that has earned it the name of Monk Vulture in many countries. The large coniferous trees, with their dense solid-looking canopies provide a good base for these giant birds to construct their huge heavy nests in. Surreal-looking orchards deserve surreal-looking birds to nest in them.

I travel onwards, passing through the scattering of villages that are all tied to the Stone Pine and Almond orchards of these richer soils. On the edge of every village, I go past the imposing evergreen cypress trees; arboreal sentries standing guard at cemeteries like dark slim fingers pointing upwards.

The road straightens out as it skirts the fringes of the plain to the north of the Salor, but just as I start to increase my speed, I spot something that makes me immediately slow down again and come to a halt in a convenient gateway. In the field opposite me, right alongside the road, there are at least sixty vultures, just seemingly standing there passing the time of day. The majority are Griffons, but there also five Blacks with them, standing noticeably taller than their tawny-coloured relatives. They are all grouped together at the top of a small rise in the field.

I put the window down, but daren't get out – I am far too close for them to tolerate my presence out of the vehicle. Instead, I take the opportunity to enjoy some roadside vulture watching. The birds initially eye my stopped vehicle with suspicious trepidation, but they gradually relax and begin to look elsewhere. I can see that they have just fed, their crops are bulging and the normally pale faces and necks of the Griffons are stained a dirty red from their recent meal.

Two Ravens appear from a hidden fold of the field, waddling into view with their typical corvid gait. Although they are the largest passerine, they are dwarfed by the vultures around them. They stop their waddling as soon as they see me, a brief look, and then they are gone; sleek shiny black wings powering them up and away. Their mistrust of humans evident in their reaction.

The vultures are loafing, resting after the feeding, allowing their food to go down before they return to the skies. I count them: sixty-three Griffon Vultures and five Black

A Black Vulture and several Griffon Vultures loafing in the landscape after feeding.

Vultures, and all just a few dozen metres away from where I am sitting. I am unable to see the carcass, which is likely to be in the fold of land from where the Ravens appeared, but the presence of sixty-eight vultures, all with bulging crops indicates to me that very little of it remains.

If the vultures had remained by the carcass to digest their meal, they would mostly likely be hidden from the road, but these birds have moved into full view of the passing traffic. This may seem odd, but what the birds have done is to opt for the security provided by the small knoll, which gives them a combination of all-round visibility and a clear downhill runway should it be required. Passing traffic is just that – passing. The mainly indifferent or unobservant motorist driving past is not considered a threat; my stopping provoked some uncertainty, but by staying in the vehicle I have become nothing more than a background object.

Occasional squabbles flare up amongst the Griffons; they are densely packed on the small rise, all wanting to take advantage of it, and the shuffling of some encroaches on the personal space of others. Wronged birds vent their anger at the insult, posturing clearly with a deliberate movement of their wings, opening them slightly and drooping them downwards, angling their neck as they do so towards the intruder in an accusing point and reinforcing their displeasure with harsh, loud hissing noises. Most of the disputes playing out in front of me are solved in this ritualised way, and the hierarchy is re-established with minimal fuss. The pecking order in a colony is reflected at a carcass, but carcasses can attract birds from many different colonies, and when this happens, it can bring equally dominant birds together in a confined space. They are no longer bickering over food, but

Vultures adopt threatening postures to reinforce the pecking order when feeding. Here a bird can be seen with outstretched wings and lowered neck and head, clearly signalling its displeasure.

space is now the objective and as I watch the vultures and their little spats, two birds take it one step further.

The drooped wings and accusatory neck of the first bird have provoked a response in kind from the second, the posturing by both now accompanied by locked stares. But this isn't about who blinks first because the blinking is part of the threat. As they stare hard at each other, the birds blink, closing their sinister-looking opaque nictating membrane across the eye in a deliberate and obvious manner. Stare, blink, stare, blink, stare, blink. Finally, the first bird has had enough of the blinking staring competition. It opens its long wings fully, and the birds either side move away with disgruntled hisses and guttural sounds. It then slowly, purposefully, raises one of its feet, showing the other bird the underside of the splayed toes and their large blunt talons. It holds the pose for several seconds, a pose that looks vaguely comical, but is full of serious intent. The second bird doesn't back down, doesn't defer, and so suddenly the first bird launches itself at the still-blinking and staring opponent, jumping into it just as the other bird reacts by jumping upwards. They bang their bodies heavily into one another, the bills of both birds flashing between them, the grunts and hisses reaching a crescendo. And then it is over. The second bird hops away slightly, and the first stands still, wings open, staring at it with now unblinking eyes. Nearby Griffons hiss at the two fighters; discontent suddenly seems rife. The birds are too full to want to fly, but evidently not too full to fight. More squabbles over space break out between the Griffons, and posturing birds make unearthly noises at each other, but eventually they settle down into an uneasy peace. Throughout it all, the Blacks have remained stationary, impassively watching their smaller relatives and their petty disputes, but now one of them decides to walk straight through the mass of argumentative Griffons, who immediately forget their differences and subserviently get out of its way. To my anthropomorphic eyes, it appears as if the Black just decided to show the rabble who the real dominant bird is.

I watch the birds for a few more minutes and then decide to head on, leaving the vultures to their fractious loafing. As the road arcs back towards the Tajo, entering dehesa briefly, I turn south to head for the Salor. But I don't head straight there; the lure of the plains is far too strong for that and, as the road emerges on to the plains, I turn off the tarmac and onto the gravelled surface of the track that loops over the vast grassland.

Sitting on a metal fence post, right alongside the track is a Hoopoe, surely the most quixotic of birds, an unrealistic, unpractical, almost fantastical-looking bird, as well as being a truly beautiful one. I pull slowly up to the post, stopping just a metre or so away from it. The sunlight highlights the soft buffish pink of the bird's chest as the bird completely disregards my presence, turning its head to the side, looking away from me as I look at it.

Hoopoe, with their hammerhead appearance, are truly unique birds.

The flattened black-spotted crest combined with the long, thin decurved bill gives the bird a unique hammerhead profile. I slowly try and reach for my camera, but the movement is noticed and the bird is away on its black and white rounded wings, a brief flappy flight before landing again on another post, flicking its crest up as it does so. I get my camera primed and slowly edge forward, but the bird no longer ignores me and flies away again, angling around and giving me a wide berth before returning to the post it was originally on. I watch it in the wing mirror for a few moments before moving onwards, trundling along the track with a big broad smile on my face.

A Little Owl is watching me intently with wide staring yellow eyes burning bright, relentless in their focus. I can't help but to stare back, transfixed by the big eyes of this little owl. Sitting on a telegraph pole, it follows my movement, an avian CCTV system seemingly recording everything I do. I slow down and come to a stop and sit there out on the plain watching the watcher watch me. A group of Calandra Lark fly up from the field behind the pole on which the owl sits and I follow them as they fly low over the field and then drop back down into the grasses. I turn my attention back to the owl to find that it is still looking at me, observing my presence in its world. I decide to leave it on its lookout, feeling its eyes following me as I continue along the track.

On the crest of the next low rise, I spot a distant Great Bustard, their more sober winter appearance making them harder to spot against the background of plains. I get out the car to watch them and, as I do, I glance back from whence I came – the owl is still on the pole and is still staring. As I focus on the bustards I realise that there are more than I first saw. I tally up twenty-seven of these large bulky birds, a winter group walking across the plains, feeding on small seeds and always nervously looking about. They are already moving away from me, even though I am several hundred metres away. They don't waste energy flying; they just steadily walk away, disappearing one by one into the undulations of the plain.

I stretch my legs a bit, walk across the track and onto the grass verge, and head for the fence to scan the other side of the track. A sudden explosion of rapid movement from right in front of me stops me dead and makes my heart jump, startled by a startled hare. An Iberian Hare, perfectly camouflaged in the grasses, has lost its nerve and bolted. A blur of long legs and long ears races off through the long grass and onto the hard, open running surface of the track. It is lightning quick as it races away, covering many tens of metres across the gravel before suddenly swerving left, off the track and into the sanctuary of green on the other side at a blistering pace. The hare is gone in seconds, whilst I stand rooted to the spot, my heart still pounding with the shock of its sudden emergence from right in front of me. It is only after it has gone that I feel able to react.

The slurred, almost drunken, gull-like calls of Pin-tailed Sandgrouse catch my ear and I see a group of them flying on fast wings, low in the sky, beautiful white undersides fringed with black wing tips and brown chests; their eponymous rear end so distinctive against the blue sky. They make constant changes of direction as they fly, sometimes splitting the group of twelve into smaller factions, but always reuniting as they race, pigeon-like, above the plains. As I watch these beautiful birds, I feel my heart rate calming down – a restoration of tranquillity after the jolt of the hare.

The wide-open nature of the landscape lends itself to serenity. The gently rolling grasslands surround me and the distant hills create far horizons below the pale blue, untroubled sky. There are no sounds apart from the occasional calls of birds carrying on the light wind, a wind that gently tickles the longer stems into soft movements. The plains look healthy; the downpours of November have saturated the hard, dry soils and the grasses have responded. They are now verdant carpets flush with growth that are occasionally interrupted by rows of jagged dark rocks breaking through the surface. These rocks are the dog's teeth in the local farmer's terminology, lurking in the grasses ready to bite an unwary combine harvester during next year's hay cut. But the stone teeth are dormant in the winter and there is no machinery in use for them to bite; instead, they make useful vantage points and I can see that one of them has a small bird using it for that very purpose, perched on the broken top of the rock, watching out over the grassy expanse in front of it.

A Griffon Vulture alongside one of the many Dientes de Perro or dog's teeth that pepper the landscape.

A Merlin, the smallest falcon and not much bigger than a Blackbird with a mini-Peregrine shape, is sitting there patiently and unobtrusively waiting for an opportunity. It is a female, her dark colouration and clearly marked five-bar gate pattern of the tail distinctive. She is a traveller from the north of Europe, possibly Scandinavian, she could be British, she could even be Icelandic in origin. Wherever she is from, she is here wintering in Iberia to exploit the concentrated gatherings of small birds that, like her, are escaping the colder weather of the northern climes. The plains are full of potential Merlin food – masses of Meadow Pipits, large numbers of larks and big numbers of small birds, all of which are an irresistible attraction for the little predator on the jagged geological tooth.

After a few minutes of calm repose, she suddenly slips off the erect stone, flying low, hugging the ground just inches from the grass below her. Her rapid wing beats propel her along at a steadily increasing pace before she really hits the accelerator, becoming a brown blur dashing across the plains. Small birds rise in panic from the grasses in front of her, scattering everywhere as the bullet-fast raptor enters their midst. It is too fast for me to really follow what happens, but the small falcon continues onwards, slower now, hugging the contours as she goes, her target missed. She disappears from view and is swallowed up by the vastness of the land; she will have to try again.

The sun is beginning to approach the horizon of hills to the west, and already Cranes are in the air, leaving the dehesa and heading to their roost sites. Faint trumpeting calls just about reach me on the lightly moving air as I watch their undulating lines across the reddening blue. I head back towards the car, my lengthening shadow testament to the shortness of the days at this time of year.

A weak mist hangs over the surface of the reservoir, a gossamer of moisture thinly veiling the water below it, obscuring the forms on its surface. A group of small ducks makes for the cover of some grassy vegetation growing at the water's edge, vanishing into it before I can get my binoculars up and focused. I wait patiently for some movement and eventually the back end of one of the ducks moves slowly into view, the pale yellow undertail of a Teal, a diagnostic glimpse as the bird shifts position and is again obscured.

The ducks are nervous in unfamiliar areas as they move around the country on their winter journey. But other winter visitors are more confident and not afraid to be seen – a group of Lapwing are having a nap on some exposed mud, their bills tucked into their wings as their long feathery crests sway gently in the breeze. They are enjoying some downtime, but not all the waders are sleeping. Spread out around the reservoir, in a somewhat random scattering, a handful of Common Snipe are methodically probing the mud at the water's edge with their improbably long bills. They pause their probing as I go past, confident in their stripy plumage, and as soon as they have judged that I have moved beyond them, they resume their work along the narrow strip of wet mud.

I can see a Red Kite further along the track, taking an obvious interest in the field beyond the wire fence. It circles broadly on its long graceful wings that take it out over the track and the reservoir edge beyond. Even in the dull light, the bird's rufous colouring on its underside and the rudder-like forked tail are immediately obvious. The bigger and more graceful relative of the Black Kite maintains a steady height as it turns clockwise in the air, only gaining height as my progress along the track takes me nearer to it. The kite is reluctant to leave and still gains height whilst keeping an eye on the field below. The field undulates away from the dip in the landscape in which the reservoir lies. Within it are parallel lines of short plastic tree tubes crowned with the spiky branches of young Evergreen Oaks, their small green leaves heavily topiaried by browsing animals that the barbed wire fence clearly does not exclude. Between these neat lines, an unkempt mat of tangled grasses dominates, and some way off from where I am standing, I see the long dark neck, topped with an equally dark head, of a Black Vulture poking up through the tangle.

It is a young bird with a black neck and a full crop of black hair-like down on its head; its blue cere behind the bill noticeable against the darkness of the bird's appearance. There are no other birds that I can see on the ground and, above me, only the Red Kite is showing any interest. The dehesa, which is an untidy-looking field full of plastic-tubed trees at the moment, does not have any livestock and so what the Black Vulture has come down for is unclear. What is clear, is that the young scavenger has seen me. Its jet-coloured eyes are fixed firmly on me and I daren't move. The bird is too close to the track for me to continue my walk. I stand there watching the bird watching me, and then I slowly start to inch backwards. I don't want to force the bird to fly if I can help it, but my actions are in vain – as soon as I start to move the big raptor moves too. A pair of huge black wings appear out of the grasses, pointing almost straight up in a tight V-shape, the head lowers and turns away from me as the bird powers the wings down to generate tremendous lift. It manages to get airborne on the first downward stroke, its legs just inches above the young trees. Again, the wings flap; the noise of the air being pushed downwards by them is audible as I stand on the track. The grasses are buffeted by the air current created by the rising vulture. Another tremendous deep flap and the bird is now up, using its wings to catch the air, using that air to move off, to put distance between us. I watch guiltily as the bird powers itself away from me, expending valuable energy to do so.

The Red Kite decides to pile on the guilt. I had stopped watching it as soon as I had seen the vulture, but now it returns into view. Ever the opportunist, the kite swoops in on those long wings, dropping its legs to snatch at the grass below, rising again as it flies on, carrying the torn body of a dead rabbit away in its talons. Above it, the Black Vulture is now steadily gaining height on broad flat wings. It is looking down at the scene playing out below it and I can feel those dark black eyes staring hard at me.

Despite their huge domineering size, Black Vultures feed frequently on small carcasses; the more gregarious-feeding Griffons wouldn't come down to such a meal, preferring larger mammals such as deer and livestock. But the Black is happy to dine alone and the carcasses of small animals are a vital food source that it is ready to be exploited. Before disease wiped out a large proportion of Iberia's endemic rabbit population, rabbits were probably this huge bird's principle food source; since then it has had to adapt its diet to counter-effect the loss of the lagomorphs. The large extensive farming of this vulture landscape and the increasing populations of both wild deer and wild pig have meant that plenty of alternative food can be found. A Black Vulture can be all alone scavenging the carcass of a small rabbit one week; the next it could be keeping a mass of Griffons at bay whilst it rips open the hide of a large Charolais bull.

They don't just confine themselves to mammals. I have seen a Black Vulture feeding on a large dead fish left stranded on the shore of a reservoir, something that the smaller Egyptian Vulture will also readily feed on. Elsewhere in their range they have been reported feeding on reptiles, especially tortoises and terrapins, and here in Extremadura I caught one on a camera trap feeding on the small carcass of a chicken I had left out for nocturnal mammals, such as the Beech Marten. Being opportunistic in its diet has ensured that this mighty bird has not just survived the loss of a large part of its natural diet, but it has also been able to expand its numbers, especially now that the threat of persecution has greatly diminished.

The low sun of the afternoon casts chill shadows of the trees of the dehesa across the stony track. The air temperature follows the sun as it begins to descend, with any warmth felt earlier proving to be ephemeral beneath the now cloudless sky and the lack of any insulating cloud signifying that a frost is likely tonight.

A scattering of cows, rich brown in colour, meander through the widely spaced, twisted stems of the oaks, pausing to feed on the grasses as they go. Groups of Spotless Starlings follow them assiduously, fast black shapes feeding amongst the feet of the cattle, snaffling anything disturbed by the lumbering bovines. A flock of Corn Bunting get up from the longer grasses that demarcate a wetter area of terrain, flying away in a mass of dry calls and fast wings. Cranes scrawl their way across the sky to the west, dark silhouettes against the lowering sun, announcing to all that they are returning to their roost with trumpeting calls that echo across the landscape.

To the east, a bird hovers over the dehesa, working hard in the unstirring air to maintain its position, to keep its head stock-still as it focuses on the grassland below, waiting for the hint of movement that will betray the presence of its hoped-for meal. This is the classic hunting technique of the kestrel, but the bird employing it in the late afternoon is no fan-tailed falcon. Lit up perfectly by the descending sun, the hoverer gleams seemingly pure white against the dark green background of the manipulated oak canopies.

The bird is facing my direction, its white underside reflecting the sun's light so brightly that the black wing tips aren't immediately obvious to the naked eye. It shifts position in the air momentarily, revealing its upper side to be a delicate pale grey, offset with black epaulette patches that give this bird its name of Black-shouldered Kite. This short-tailed, compact raptor suddenly folds up its proportionally long wings and plunges downward, disappearing from view behind the oaks. I don't need to wait long to see it again. It reappears flying powerfully up and out of the trees, its clutched feet tell of the success of its dive as it flies in my general direction before pitching into the top of a large domed oak.

The small kite sits in the tree, a vision of beauty with its sharp designer label-like plumage, the large, almost owl-like head home to two eyes that burn like red embers in the sunlight. A quick look around and then it lowers its head eagerly, carefully dismembering the small mammal grasped tightly in its talons. As the fur drifts slowly in the air about it, the bird pauses repeatedly in its feeding to look all around it, wary of thieves and threats, its gloriously red eyes meet mine for a moment, burning my own retinas with their intensity, before the bird looks away and continues its meal.

Hypnotised by the small raptor, I watch the bird methodically consume its catch, gulping down the last of it in a quick head jerking movement. Sated, the bird sits in the tree for several more minutes as the light noticeably fades, preening briefly and combing its bill through the feathers of its wings, one after another. It sits still for a few more minutes, and then, after a quick rouse, stretching it's feathers out, it jumps upwards from its perch and opens its wings to take to the air again. It initially flies upwards before gliding on raised wings across the dehesa, its whiteness continuing to glow in the dusk-laden air as it flies away from me. Realising the time, feeling the chill and seeing the coming darkness, I head off along the track, walking briskly to generate some internal warmth as I make my way back towards the already twinkling lights of the village.

I pause to look out over the river by the granary at the edge of the village, my breath forming wisps of cloud. Night has now fallen and only a faint remnant of glow is left on the western horizon and the stars are already emerging in their millions. A clear night reflected in the black still of the water, the reed-dominated margins of which rustle continuously, notifying to all that listen that they are full of life. Somewhere from the village, the shrill hissing call of a Barn Owl drifts in the cold air, an ominous reminder that the cloak of night doesn't bring safety.

JANUARY

The ice-coated puddles crack loudly under my feet as I walk out of the village. Frosted spider webs hang heavy in the grasses flanking the track, iced silken adornments testament to the sub-zero temperature. The cold air, bracing against the skin of my face, is a world away from the burning heat of August, when even the thought of a puddle, let alone an iced one, seemed impossible.

Straggly broken flocks of Spotless Starlings pour forth from the sanctuary of the village as the sky in the east brightens with the promise of a new day. They are not heading to the fields to feed, not yet. They are racing to claim the best spot from which to welcome the sun as it rises.

The village and its reservoir sit in a shallow broad geographical bowl in the landscape, a subtle depression in the terrain that means the first of the winter sun's rays don't reach it for a few minutes after the golden orb breaks into the sky. The tardiness of the sun in reaching the rooftops of the village is what drives the starlings to abandon it as dawn approaches.

On a frozen cold January morning those few minutes of delay are evidently not endurable for these gregarious birds, and so they head to where they know they will be amongst the first to feel the welcome warmth of the sun after the long dark cold of the night before. There are several pylons dotted around the reservoir, a network of buzzing, flowing electricity that powers our human world. Metallic towers, ugly scaffolds, angular reminders of our domination. But, for a few minutes, as a new day dawns, they become a power source for others.

The starlings land, one after another, on the upper arms of the structure; small dark shapes jostling and shuffling along the horizontals. Above them, a bigger shape already sits in the prime position, a Red Kite, waiting patiently for the imminent warmth of the new day to arrive. Starlings and kites are odd bedfellows – the smaller birds are generally noisily intolerant of the presence of a much larger predator, but in the quest for the dawning sun it appears that all hostilities have been suspended. The light arrives, bathing the kite in its glow and soon the starlings are basking too, chattering loudly as the sunlight coats them with much-needed warmth.

In the sierra, a pair of Black Vultures sit in their nest tree, two dark masses absorbing the sunlight as it spreads across the hillside. They are standing on the edge of the huge bulk of sticks that make up the nest, their large feet hidden by their insulating posture. Spanish Sparrows, mere specks of birds in comparison, sit around the giant pair, using the elevated platform much like the starlings on the pylon a few kilometres to the north.

The sun rapidly climbs and soon its light reaches the multifaceted cliffs of the quarry, highlighting the hunched figures of the Griffons spaced along its ledges. Their heads are tucked into their fluffed-out ruffs, motionless in the morning sunshine, whilst around them the multitude of smaller birds sharing this rocky hole with them get on with their busy lives.

One of the Black Vultures in the tree shifts sideways slightly, unfurls a wing and nibbles at the shafts of the exposed feathers. The unfurling of the huge wing causes momentary panic in the sparrows, scattering them asunder. The vulture doesn't notice, it just quells the annoying itch with its bill and then folds its wing back up again. It looks around the nest tree and then at its mate alongside. Another day in the vulture landscape has dawned.

The calls of unseen distant cranes haunt the air, white clouds move hurriedly through the blue sky, powered along by an increasingly strong cold wind that negates the warmth of the sun. The tall, unkempt stems of the *Retama* scrub clatter into themselves, waving briskly in the breeze. The Crested Larks stay low in the moving grasses, occasionally leaping into the flow, allowing themselves to be whipped away by it before regaining some measure of control and landing dozens of metres away from where they began.

A Black Vulture is up high, watching all as it crosses the sky on its broad flat wings, wings that remain unflapped. Watching it gives the impression of calmness, but the larks show the turbulent truth, but still the vulture remains unflappable in its journey. It uses and takes advantage of the wind, gliding through it at just the angle required to allow the constant correct flow of air over and under the black sail-like wings. It maintains its altitude, speed and direction with small movements of the splayed primary feathers and slight adjustments to the angle and position of its mighty wings.

The larks embark on random journeys; the vulture does not. It is the embodiment of control, exploiting the fast-moving air, travelling many kilometres and covering thousands of hectares and all for a minimal energy cost. Flight is energy demanding, birds that have to flap their wings to maintain their altitude in flight use up their energy reserves much faster than those that use alternative flying techniques. Soaring is one of those alternative techniques and vultures are absolute masters at it.

The big broad wings of a vulture require a lot of energy to flap, but they are perfect for soaring, perfect for catching the air currents and riding them to gain height. Those same wings, held in a slightly different pose, are also perfect for gliding through the air, just as the Black Vulture above the swaying *Retama* is doing. The vulture's aerodynamics help to minimise the inevitable height loss as the bird glides, cutting through the air on outstretched wings. It uses gravity and air movement as its power source, rather than costly muscles. Being literate in the language of air enables the bird to find the currents, to find the rising columns that can take it higher again. This allows it to cover vast distances to scour the landscape for food without having to burn valuable energy reserves.

For many birds, the act of flying means they have to substantially increase their metabolic rate to cope with the increased energy demands of flight. For some, this means an increase of sixteen times the metabolic rate required when perched, but for the flight-

A young Black Vulture on the ground, their keen eye helps them spot even small carcasses.

efficient vultures it is less than one and a half times. It is no surprise to learn that the flight abilities of vultures have been, and are still being, studied by scientists and engineers working in the aeronautical industry. Energy efficiency is becoming ever more important in our modern world and vultures are the ultimate low-energy flyers to learn from.

The Black Vulture's keen eye spots something down below it. The huge bird adjusts its flight posture and banks round to have another look. It circles the area over the minor road and the large wide strip of scrubby grass that separates the tarmac from the fields beyond. A fox carcass lies crumpled a few metres from the edge of the tarmac. The bird circles it one more time before it lowers its legs and starts to descend.

The Black Vulture is distributed along a narrow band of latitude running from Iberia in the west through to the Korean peninsula in the east. It is not uniformly distributed within this area, being sadly absent from much of its previous range in Europe, but it is coming back in places. Numerous conservation and reintroduction projects are ongoing, working to return these giants of the bird world to the skies of Europe where they belong. Further east, they are found at higher altitudes and their range includes the highest areas of our planet – Tibet and Nepal. In these countries, these impressive birds can be found breeding at over four thousand metres in altitude, patrolling the alpine meadows and breeding in the montane forests. Climbers on Everest have seen the birds fly past them at about seven thousand metres, an altitude where most human climbers are forced to use oxygen tanks to sustain them. These high, oxygen-depleted altitudes are dangerous places for humans, but not for the Black Vulture.

Their feathers insulate them against the cold air, much like the climber's state-of-the-art clothing, but it is their blood that is the key to their ability to cope with the conditions. It contains a specialised type of haemoglobin that enables them to absorb enough oxygen from the thin air to be able to fly in their usual efficient manner. The lack of oxygen at these altitudes kills people, but the vulture simply glides on through, perfectly evolved to deal with it.

Another vulture takes this adaptation even further. The Rüppell's Vulture, that occasional visitor from Africa, also has specialised blood and is regularly recorded flying at similar heights to the Black in the Himalayas. But they have also gone higher, much higher. In 1973, a commercial airliner flying over the Ivory Coast struck a Rüppell's. The collision caused major damage to the plane and forced it to make an emergency landing. The height of the collision was over eleven thousand metres, that's over eleven kilometres above sea level or, if you prefer, seven miles up.

This incredible altitude gave that unfortunate Rüppell's Vulture the status of being the highest flying bird ever recorded. Vultures really are the ultimate flying machines.

Vultures circling against a sky that forebodes rain.

The wind is beginning to ease as I look out over the rugged, ridged countryside of the northern Sierra de San Pedro. The clouds have started to amalgamate into larger masses of whiteness gradually hemming in the areas of blue. Much further to the west the skies are thickening over Portugal; warmer air is beginning to seep in and with it the promise of some more rain. For the moment the blue sky holds firm, the greyer, water-laden clouds are still a long way off and I decide to continue my walk along the stony track.

About fifty metres in front of me a low-slung, elongated dark shape slinks across my path – an Egyptian Mongoose briefly showing itself before vanishing into the mass of scrubby vegetation lining the track, its long tail with the tufted mass of hair at its end is the last part of it to be swallowed up by the wall of leaves. It may be out of sight, but I still know where it is, its unseen course through the security of the Cistus plotted by the urgent, harsh warning calls of numerous small birds that inhabit it. This misnamed mammal, long thought of as an alien invader from across the Mediterranean, has now been finally identified as a native species. DNA studies show that it has been in Iberia, separate from its North African cousin, for at least thirty thousand years. It belongs here.

Wary of being exposed in the open, most views of this diurnal predatory mammal consist of a brief dash from cover to cover. Persecuted by us and hunted by others, mongoose are wise to keep a low profile, especially here within the Imperial realm. Sure enough, it is not long before the regal rulers of this wild landscape appear. I spot them both at the same time – the male and female Spanish Imperial Eagles whose territory I am in the heart of. Classic long-winged, long-tailed eagle shapes, they are more rectangular in the wings than the similar sized Golden. These birds are gliding along the top of the far ridge, the slightly smaller male above and just ahead of the female. They begin to soar upwards, circling together and rapidly gaining height. Suddenly, one of the pair breaks out of the soar and stoops hard, wings tucked back, the white leading edge gleaming in the light as the bird plummets downwards, barking loudly. It is all so quick, but the barking call registers with me that this is no hunting stoop – this is aggression.

A Griffon Vulture, flapping hard, evidently aware of the impending eagle, appears from the vicinity of the Imperial's nest tree. This most efficient of flyers suddenly looks cumbersome as it flaps hard trying to get up speed. The eagle is on it in a split second, throwing its legs forward, lethal talons brought to the fore, striking at the much bigger vulture. It hits it across the back and the vulture manages to do just enough to avoid the full impact of the raging Imperial by sharply turning at the last moment. The eagle powers itself upward and banks back around; it is not done yet. Deep, powerful wing beats propel it rapidly through the air in pursuit of the Griffon, barking continuously as it closes in on the vulture. The second eagle suddenly appears, joining the fray. The vulture, working hard and flapping those huge wings in an attempt to gain height, can't out fly these two masters of high-speed pursuit and is struck again across the back by the first eagle as it blazes past it, angrily barking out its call as it does so.

The vulture feels the impact, drops downwards slightly and starts to bank around to the right. The second eagle now screams towards it, flashing its talons in a clear warning of murderous intent as it powers past the hapless vulture before it arcs back around and above it, joining its mate in vociferous disapproval of the fleeing vulture's presence. Both eagles begin once more to gain height, but not to attack. The vulture has rapidly left the scene, still flapping hard, and the eagles, victorious, turn back towards the area in which their nest lies.

The Imperial's breeding season is about to begin in earnest. Last year's nest has already been refurbished with new material added, egg laying is still three or more weeks away, but they have become fiercely protective of the site and will not tolerate trespassers, especially Griffons.

Griffons have taken over Imperial nests elsewhere, but with the Griffons almost about to lay, I don't think the vanquished vulture had usurpation on its mind. Instead, I think it naively thought it could help itself to one of the branches placed on the eagle's nest to add to its own on the nearby ledges. The eagles quickly disabused it of that idea.

Gathering nest material can be a difficult business for birds that need large sticks to construct their large nests. There can be intense competition for the best materials, and the temptation to pick up ones already gathered is an obvious one, but stealing from eagles is not to be recommended. Looking up at the ledges I can see several Griffon Vultures standing by their own nests, perhaps standing guard against the potential of pilfering neighbours.

Sometimes vultures will snap nest material straight off the tree. I have seen them fly towards dead branches sticking out of a tree's canopy, grabbing them with their feet and using their momentum and their weight to break the branch off the tree. This comes with a risk, however, and most prefer to pick up branches already broken off. The tall alien Eucalyptus trees planted here, and across this region in the sixties and seventies, provide a steady supply of broken branches and many of these will have been used in the construction of the nests dotted along the cliff face in front of me. Within the next week or so, the female Griffons will lay their single egg in these cupped structures and begin the long incubation of it.

One of the eagles is still visible in the air, circling high over the nesting site. Further to the east a large flock of birds, several thousand strong is making its way towards the sierra, and their presence will have been undoubtedly noticed by the Imperial. Woodpigeons winter in Extremadura in vast numbers and between one and three million birds come to the region during January and February, descending from northern Europe to take advantage of the huge acorn crop ripening in the dehesa.

It is not unusual to see several thousand pigeons in one flock, and the flock that is heading this way looks to be at least three thousand birds strong. It is an impressive sight to see, and an impressive sound to hear – densely packed birds, pigeon wings beating with their characteristic noise, soughing air flowing over and under the birds. A mass of soft grey passes high overhead and, as they go, so the sound of their noisy flight diminishes, growing quieter as the birds head off towards the dehesa beyond. Huge numbers of plump fleshy pigeons are bound to attract attention.

I try to locate the Imperial again, expecting to find it powering towards the passing flock; instead, I find the compact shape of the eternal pigeon pursuer – the blunt short tail and long, sharply pointed wings of a Peregrine. Shallow, stiff wing beats drive the bird on as it follows the pigeons ominously, climbing all the time, deliberately positioning itself above the flock. But before the inevitable strike happens, the terrain intervenes as first the flock and then the follower disappear over the ridged skyline in front of me.

My frustration at missing the hunter hunting is alleviated by the mesmerising sound of cranes, and I turn to look towards the glowering skies of the west where a linear ribbon of seventeen birds is making its way through the sky. Long-necked, long-winged and long-legged with stretched shapes and far-carrying calls, cranes are beautiful birds and they have a hypnotic quality, entrancing you into watching them.

The spell is broken by fat, heavy drops of rain. The blue sky above has lost the fight, the once-white clouds are now united in grey coverage. I walk rapidly back up the track, glancing quickly at the vultures on the cliffs, they have seen it coming and have hunkered down, heads resting on their shoulders, staring out at the coming weather. By the time I get to the car I am soaked.

The weather front carrying the rain lingers until the following morning, but once it stops, the skies soon clear and the blue expanse returns as I head out of the village once more. Everything feels refreshed by the rain, the cold air of yesterday morning has been replaced by a moderate warmth. It is ideal walking weather and I take advantage of it, heading north out of the village and following the track that accesses the stone wall-partitioned grazing fields that act as an agricultural buffer between the village and the dehesa beyond.

The first green fields, dotted with yellow by the small flowers of a wild rocket, are full of Meadow Pipits and, as I get further from the village, further from the noises of human life, they are joined by Lapwing and Golden Plover, two species of wader that are abundant winterers on the grass fields and plains. The Golden Plover stand motionless as I walk by, confident in their subdued winter plumage; the Lapwings, which are much more showy with a mixture of darkness and white, a touch of iridescence on the wings and back, and a rear-pointing thin crest, seem much more jumpy, and walk away with quick steps, watching warily. Nervousness is the price of their flamboyant plumage.

Several Corn Buntings are singing in the sunshine and use the angular metal posts jutting up from the rounded stones of the walls as the stage for their rehearsals for the singing contests of the soon-to-be-with-us spring. Their jangly songs are interspersed with sorties to the ground to feed, legs dangling below them as they fly on fast wings. Stonechats lay claim to other posts, standing proudly, black head, white collar and orange fronted – always busy, always alert. Beneath the posts, Crested Larks pick their way through the grasses of the fields, whilst others run along the side of the track in front of me.

Lines of gulls go by overhead. Lesser Black-backs overwinter far away from the coast and roost in their hundreds on the vast reservoirs of the region. They are high up and the

A male Stonechat looking resplendent. A very common bird of the countryside in Extremadura.

white underside of their wings reflect the light. In contrast, a young Black Vulture glides by below the high lines of gulls, its black wings absorbing the light rather than reflecting it. The gulls with steady wing beats; the vulture on level, unflapping wings.

Out towards the east, near where the main road leaves the village behind, a Common Kestrel is hovering, the windhover hanging in the air, tail fanned, wings working, head held perfectly still and focusing hard on the ground below. It lowers its head, tucks its wings in and drops down a few metres, before opening the wings up again, angling its body into the wind, defying gravity once more as it hangs in the air. The wings again fold back, this time with more purpose, and the bird dives rapidly, dropping out of my field of view, before reappearing again several seconds later, flying up and away on clipped wing beats, the normally sleek lines of the falcon's underside broken by a bulging foot, clutched tightly around its mammalian victim.

The geometric network of stone-walled fields lies before me as I look back towards the village nestling in its dip. Some way beyond the terracotta-coloured roofs, the regular line of the sierra forms a high horizon, blocking out the landscape beyond. There are several Griffon Vultures spaced across the sky and, as I watch these, I spot another raptor, but this one much closer and low down over the fields in front of me.

A beautiful, immaculate adult male Hen Harrier ghosting across the stone-walled pastures on its elegant long black-tipped wings. The Golden Plover are not so confident in the presence of this flapping and gliding hunter, taking to the air as one and moving in a tight flock on fast wings, putting distance between themselves and the harrier. But the Hen Harrier is not interested in their activity, He ignores their panic and continues his untroubled slow flight over the fields. The raised V-shape of the wings show off the plumage of the bird – a palette of pale blue-grey, white and black; a list of dull-sounding colours combined to create one of the most beautiful birds there is.

It banks away from me, heading back towards the village, and continues its quartering flight across the fields, sweeping up and over the outlying buildings, dropping back down again and flying low over the grasses. Its head always fixed on the ground beneath it. The curious owl-like face is a perfectly evolved parabolic receiver that relays the faintest of sounds to its ears, whilst the sharp eyes seek the telltale movement. Flap, flap, glide – a deliberately patient and slow flight searching for small mammals, and flying just a few metres away from the first of the houses. A bird so heavily persecuted in my home country, but living and hunting alongside us in this one.

Eventually the pale hunter gives up its search. It gains height, flaps its long wings and heads off to the east of the village to chance its arm on the fields there. Turning around again, I head away from the village and follow the track as it continues up the shallow incline. Spotless Starlings, less glossy in their winter plumage, are busily probing the short turf in a field that has recently had cattle. Dozens of pale black birds chatter continuously to one another as they jab their bills into the ground, somehow finding time to look for insect larvae between their varied vocalisations.

The next field holds the dried-out, hollowed-out shell of a cow that has evidently been there for several days. Taut, tattered hide covers the rib cage, giving some shape to an otherwise broken heap of what is now just bone and hair. The long necks of the Griffons are ideal for reaching deep within a carcass, picking it clean from the inside, emptying out the carcass of everything edible. A few tawny-coloured feathers are caught in the trampled grasses, broken and torn; they haven't been moulted, they have been ripped out, ripped out by other vultures, jostling for the best position and resorting to yanking at the feathers of the other birds, grabbing them with their strong bills and pulling hard to ensure they get there.

The consumed cow's remains are lying in the exact centre of the field, it has been placed there deliberately to be devoured, put in a position that grants the vultures the easiest of access and, more importantly for these carrion feeders, allows them to feed with confidence. The first vultures that attend a recently discovered animal spend several minutes circling above it, assessing the situation. They are nervous of landing in a setting that not only makes it difficult for the birds to rapidly take off again, but also where their visibility is heavily compromised. That initial circling is picked up by the others in the visibility chains, but it is only when those first birds are satisfied and start to descend that the birds watching from afar begin to get really interested. If the circling birds don't like

This Griffon Vulture is showing the long neck of the species, which is ideal for reaching deep inside a large carcass.

the lay of the land, they will move on and the others will not come. As a result, carcasses against stone walls are likely to be left for far longer than carcasses in the middle of fields. The longer it is left, the more it will start to decay and, despite Darwin's assertion that vultures 'wallow in putridity', these birds prefer their meat fresh. If there are other options available, a long-dead rotting carcass in a hard-to-access spot is likely to remain untouched. The farmers and livestock owners are aware of this; they know that a bit of effort on their part will rapidly speed up the free sanitation service provided by the birds.

Following the discovery of Bovine Spongiform Encephalopathy (BSE) in cattle, regulations were drawn up by the European Union (EU) to prohibit carcasses being left out in fields, even where vultures, nature's very own sanitation team, rapidly removed them and any disease reservoir that they held. These regulations came into force in 2001, meaning that farmers had to dispose of carcasses by having them physically removed and burnt at incinerators, an extremely costly method both in terms of money and in energy expended. It also meant that the vultures potentially lost an enormous food resource.

In Extremadura, where the cattle farming is extensive and the distances between towns, cities and the countryside are large, not much really changed. If a cow died in the middle of one of the huge fields on the plains, the vultures would find it and remove it long before any collection vehicle turned up. But if an animal had fallen in a more awkward situation, near a building or in a stone-walled corner, then the farmers were now legally required to dispose of it by official and expensive means. Across the border in neighbouring Portugal, the farming is not so spread out. The towns and cities are much closer to the countryside and this meant that following regulations was carried out more efficiently, resulting in a huge drop in available carcasses for the vultures to feed upon.

Meanwhile, conservationists in many countries were extremely worried about the implications of these new regulations for vultures, and other scavengers. They lobbied hard, presenting good sound scientific research to show that when it came to sanitation and the efficient removal of carcasses, no human response came anywhere near being as effective as the one already provided for free by vultures. The EU understood this and changed its regulation, allowing the conservation of scavenging birds, such as vultures, to be considered and permitting individual countries to decide on whether carcasses could be left or not.

As a result, in the majority of the Spanish countryside, home to about ninety per cent of Europe's vultures, carcasses can be left out for the vultures to deal with. But in neighbouring Portugal, well within the foraging ranges of many of the vultures in Extremadura, the authorities still require the removal of livestock carcasses from the fields.

Lines drawn on maps and international borders are very much a human concept and are not something that we expect wildlife to comprehend. However, recent scientific research has shown that vultures seem to have learnt just where those lines are drawn. Over seventy Spanish Griffon and Black Vultures were tagged with GPS devices in areas where the birds were expected to forage in both countries, crossing the international border on a regular basis. The border between the two countries is mainly demarcated by river valleys; there are no geological barriers, no large changes in land use to act as a physical barrier to these birds. For a vulture, crossing into Portugal from Spain should be no different to crossing the Rio Salor that separates the Sierra de San Pedro from the plains. It should be a frequent occurrence every day.

But the results of the GPS tagging paint another picture. Quite literally. When the movements of the vultures were plotted onto a map, they showed that the vultures were hardly ever crossing the boundary. In some parts of Spain, especially in the vulture landscape of Extremadura, the movements drawn onto the map delineated the border almost exactly. The Spanish side was coloured with bird movements, whilst the Portuguese

A Griffon Vulture sailing the air currents on its broad wings, constantly reading the landscape beneath.

side was mainly blank. The birds have recognised where the boundaries are, not because of politics, but because of food availability.

The vultures of Spain rarely cross the border because there is no benefit to them doing so. Vultures are efficient in all that they do. The difference in agricultural practice between the two countries has created a situation where a political boundary has become an ecological barrier. It is a situation that will hopefully be changed in the future as more pressure is put upon the Portuguese authorities to relax their regulations.

I leave the ex-cow behind me and follow the track as it crests the hill and begins to swing back around to the village, giving me a panorama of the countryside and the houses snugly set within it. The larks, the buntings and the Stonechats accompany me along the track. Far away, beyond the village, more cranes are crossing the sky; elsewhere, the long wings of Red Kites can be seen over the dehesa running south to the sierra. Above them all, dotted throughout the sky, are numerous Griffon Vultures, spreading out over the landscape on their broad wings, sailing on the air currents, ever ready to engage in some carcass removal.

FEBRUARY

Spring comes early in this vulture landscape. As I leave the house for a morning walk around the reservoir, the first Barn Swallows of the year, simple graceful motions in the air, dash over the rooftops, snatching small flies as they go. A male, with resplendent tail streamers on show, arcs his flight down to a television aerial, bringing his iridescent beauty to the mundane. He sings his twittering song, laying claim to the site below where the dried-out, crumbled remnants of last year's nest remain.

The morning sun is shining brilliantly, the strong light reflecting off the white walls with a dazzling intensity as I walk through the angular maze of narrow streets. Above me the swallows dance, performing elegant manoeuvres with the consummate ease of seasoned performers. These migratory marvels have travelled thousands of miles to return here to breed, bringing with them the start of a new season – the season of renewal. To emphasise the point, a male House Sparrow drops down to snatch up a small downy feather from the edge of the concrete, whisking it away – a perfect piece of lining for its grassy nest.

The swallows are not the only hirundines to return from their travels; the dry 'drrrit' calls of House Martins blend in with the livelier, more effervescent song of their relatives as I draw nearer to the edge of the village. But there is also an avian reminder that winter still lingers as a ribbon of a dozen or so cranes trumpet their way across the sky further off to the south.

A chorus of Crested Larks accompanies me as I approach the reservoir, accentuated wings blurring their shape as they perform their song flights above the vibrant grass fields below. The larks are ascending, revelling in the new warmth of the new season. As I look out over the tranquil, bucolic scene of the reservoir and its surrounding fields, a loud noisy cackle resounds across the placid water's surface, a sound that jars harshly against the melodious lark song, trampling roughshod over the tranquillity of the moment.

It takes me a minute or two to place the sound; after all it has been almost a year since I last heard it. As my mind recognises it for what it is, my eye confirms my thoughts as it registers that the bird responsible is sitting ostentatiously on a fence post down towards the water's edge. A Great Spotted Cuckoo – a bird with a plumage almost as raucous as its call. A light grey, almost silver-crested head, with a black nape and a dark grey back and wings liberally speckled with the white spots that give it its name, this long-tailed cuckoo has a creamy white underside that finishes in white feathered legs. It is a distinctive bird and its distinctive call once again rings out loudly across the reservoir. It takes to the air, flashing the speckled back and wings as it flies low over the ground before disappearing into the Olives beyond.

It is another new arrival, again so showy and so obvious but, unlike the Barn Swallow, the cuckoo will soon become much harder to find, adopting a more secretive lifestyle and somehow blending its eccentric look into the background, turning from ostentatious to unobtrusive. As a nest parasite of the ever-alert, ever-suspicious, Common Magpie, the Great Spotted Cuckoo is a bird that has to become more clandestine in its behaviour if it is going to succeed with its breeding strategy.

The reservoir mirrors the sky as the House Martins skim low across it, creating fast-moving reflections beneath them, mirror images chasing the originals across the surface. The winter rains have replenished the small reservoir and the island is again an island. But the level is still low; a bare, cracked mud fringe encircles the smooth, unblemished water and separates it from the vegetation that should be at its edge, telling of the need for more rain before the drought returns. A White Stork, accompanied by its watery image, stalks silently around the reservoir's edge, and two Teal sit nervously in the water a few metres from a group of nine loafing Lapwings with heads tucked into their wings, snoozing in the shallows, perfectly counterpointing the two duck's jumpy behaviour.

The angled metal fence posts of the reservoir's stock fence are once again sought-after property hotspots and must-have locations. Male Stonechats, puffed out with pride, sit atop them singing their squeaky songs, occasionally nipping off to snatch an insect before rapidly returning to their chosen post. Other rust-flaked posts are claimed by Corn Buntings, pouring out their tumbling jangle of notes. The voices of buntings, chats and larks merge together, songs of intent ahead of the breeding season fill the air around the reservoir, but others are indifferent to this noticeable change in behaviour. The unassuming Meadow Pipits stubbornly continue their winter foraging of the grass fields, ignoring the frivolities around them, their own spring lying much farther north and much later in the year.

A Griffon Vulture calmly glides through the air, over the scattered oaks and fields, over the glass-like reservoir, over the differing preoccupations of the birds below. It is an adult bird, the pale beak visible in the crystal-clear light. Somewhere, perhaps in the Salor valley, its mate will be on a narrow, inaccessible ledge incubating their solitary egg. The incubation period lasts for around fifty days, a long stint equally shared by the male and the female, switching the cramped nest ledge for the open sky twice a day until the middle of March, when the small chick will slowly chip its way out of the encasing calcareous shell and emerge into the vulture landscape that it will inherit.

Vulture watching allows you to see so much – the bird above me, gliding through the air with apparent zero effort, is a great lesson in aerodynamics and flight efficiency. They are demonstrators, showing those that watch just how perfectly they have evolved to master the skies. These avian leviathans rarely make early starts; they wait for the air to warm up first. As the warm air moves, it becomes a river in the sky and, just like any river, it flows in varying rates. It has slow-moving pools and fast-moving narrows with turbulent rapids but, unlike the water in a river, this flowing, moving, invisible mass does it in three dimensions. The cold February morning that dawned a few hours ago has now been transformed. The clear skies of the night before caused the temperatures to tumble, but the same clear skies now give licence to the sun to once again raise the temperature upwards. The cold chill morning of a few hours ago has been transformed into a pleasantly warm spring day.

The sun has not just warmed the air, it has also warmed the land, but not consistently. Some areas warm faster than others, the dehesa-covered landscape doesn't warm as rapidly as the overgrazed fields or the exposed areas of rock that are found breaking through the thin soils. This disparity in rates of how land warms leads to differences in the temperature of the air above it and this, in turn, leads to air movement. Where land has warmed more rapidly than in surrounding areas, thermals can occur, and these rapidly rising currents of air are frequent in our varied landscapes. We humans can't detect them, but vultures can.

The massive, broad wings of the vulture are sails evolved to catch the rising air, to take the bird upwards without the energy-zapping demands of active flapping flight. But a large sail creates drag, weighing it down and slowing it down too. The vulture overcomes this by using its primary feathers, the characteristic fingers at the end of the wings, jutting out in an apparent unkempt manner. But these feathers aren't randomly placed; they are positioned exactly to break up the surface area of the wings at the point where, if the wing ended in a smooth rounded tip, unsteady dragging turbulence would occur. They are a drag reduction system par excellence.

The aerodynamics of vultures enable them to glide across the landscape without generating drag, which would slow them down and lead to them losing height rapidly. Gravity still pulls these flyers back to earth as they glide across the landscape, but they are so efficient that they lose less than a metre of height per second and, by using the rising air currents spread across the land below them, by soaring up the upward-moving rivers of air on their broad wings, they easily counter-effect the gravitational pull. The combination of the warm air and the vultures' extraordinary aerodynamics means that these birds could, in theory at least, fly forever without needing to flap their wings. Forget the era of cheap flights, vultures take free flights and they have been doing so for millennia.

Vulture watching allows you to appreciate this; it allows you to see the physics in action. As I watched the Griffon gliding effortlessly in the bright blue sky, travelling over the reservoir, over the fields and over the village beyond, I thought of these physical processes, of exactly what was involved and how it had evolved. But by the time my mind had begun to grasp the realities of the bird's smooth flight, it had already travelled beyond my range of vision. The rivers of the sky flow fast.

All vultures exploit these rivers, all use the movement of air to minimise their own energetic costs. Recent studies of the Egyptian Vulture population in the Iberian Peninsula have revealed some remarkable data about how these smaller relatives of the Griffons and the Blacks use their own proportionally large wings to ride the currents. One bird, fitted with the latest tracking equipment, demonstrated their exploitation of the movement of air perfectly. The bird was tracked as it migrated down through Spain towards the Straits of Gibraltar, towards the short sea crossing that takes it to its wintering quarters in Africa.

Vultures can often be seen drifting over towns and villages as they follow the rivers of the air.

Crossing large bodies of water is potentially problematic for large broad-winged birds such as vultures – there are no thermals generated at sea, meaning that unless they get it right they will have to use energy-sapping powered flight to get them over it. The bird that was tracked got it right, perfectly right. Using a thermal on the Spanish side of the strait, the Egyptian climbed to over two thousand three hundred metres in altitude, a mile and a half above sea level, and then it glided on a favourable air current out across the open sea.

The fourteen kilometres of sea was crossed in just twenty-six minutes, the bird cruising across it at a speed of around twenty miles per hour, reaching the Moroccan shore of Africa at an altitude of just over one thousand one hundred metres. During its glide, the bird had lost twelve hundred metres of height, showing the importance of using the thermals in Spain to give it the height to allow it to complete the flight without flapping. I, too, can cross the Straits, following pretty much the same route, but I would have to take the ferry, powered by massive diesel engines, consuming huge amounts of energy. It would take me an hour to do so. Vultures are the ultimate carbon neutral travellers.

I first see the vultures gathering as I stroll along in the early afternoon, following the stony track that leads north out of the village and enjoying the warmth on my back and the bird song in my ears. Tens of Griffons tightly circling are forming a kettle, a kettle that increases in members as I stand watching it. A Black Vulture flies to the left of me; its course arrow-straight for the mass of vultures ahead. A quick look around the sky sees more vultures coming, homing in on the others. Some are flying low, whilst others are dropping in from great heights. I roughly work out where their focal point is and plot my route to get me to a vantage point. I set off, walking quickly, aware that more and more vultures are gathering.

The kettle has long since gone by the time I reach the place in the landscape that should give me a view out over the area where they were circling. Occasional vultures drift by overhead, showing an interest in what is going on below them. Some circle briefly, but they do not lower their legs to descend; the feast is already over and they move on. As I get nearer to where I think I want to be, I flush out a Red Kite that was sitting unseen on the stone wall and a Raven cronks loudly and deeply at me from above – both avian indications that I was right in my navigation.

I approach the crest of the rise cautiously, walking more stealthily now, not wanting to make a sudden appearance and put to flight any of the vultures that will be on the ground, perhaps only a few metres from where I will appear. I need not have worried – the birds are spread out over a field that lies a couple of hundred metres in front of where I peer cautiously over the wall. Between me and the birds are two smaller fields, both with cattle. In the field of vultures, I can see the broken remains of a carcass, the ground around it now bare and the grass trampled and battered by the feasting and fighting of the birds. Nature's clean-up squad have cleaned up a cow and it has evidently provided quite a feast, drawing in large numbers of vultures who, judging by their bulging crops, have all partaken. I quickly count the vultures that are scattered around the field – I count eighty-three Griffon Vultures and five Black Vultures, a fine gathering indeed.

The cows in the field in the foreground are uneasy and are standing together in a group eyeing the vultures with what appears to me to be morbid curiosity. They seem, in my mind at least, fascinated by the spectacle they just witnessed. Who knows what is happening in their bovine brains as they stand there chewing the cud and observing the vultures. The loud barking of a Mastiff rings out nearby causing some of the cows to run skittishly about the field, tails held upwards and back legs kicking out at imaginary foes. The noise causes disquiet in the vultures too and those on the left side of the field start hopping ungainly towards the field's centre. The head of the barking dog appears briefly over the stone wall, before a human shout commands its return. The unseen herdsman and his dog go quiet, but their presence has undoubtedly unsettled the vultures and they are suddenly alert, hunched figures no longer, their heads held high on extended necks as they look around them.

Some of the Griffons that were nearest to where the dog briefly appeared have decided they need to put some distance between themselves and where the canine was seen. Heavy with food they would prefer not to fly, but the risk of the dog appearing close to them is one they need to mitigate. They laboriously run along the ground flapping their broad wings, some glide just above the grass for a few metres before landing again, but others do get up a bit higher, flapping their wings with real effort initially, only to fly a short distance before landing on the far side of the field. But one vulture goes further, flying past the others. It banks back around again, but instead of rejoining the vultures it lands in one of the fields nearer to me, the one where all the cows are.

The Griffon doesn't appear alarmed at being in the field on its own and settles down into the typical loafing vulture pose of folded wings and hunched back, mirroring exactly the pose of the birds on the other side of the stone wall. At first the cows in the field seem disinterested in its presence; no doubt more concerned by the possibility of the large dog returning. But slowly their curious nature draws them towards the large tawny colour bird that is digesting its meal a few tens of metres away from them. One cow boldly walks towards the bird, only to be met by the classic vulture threat display normally used when arguing over access rights to a carcass. The vulture opens its wings and droops them downwards to give the appearance of being larger than it is. At the same time, it extends its neck and head towards the inquisitive bovine and hisses loudly and menacingly at it.

It is too much for the inquisitive cow, which turns and, with a raised tail, quickly returns to its companions. But it is only a temporary victory for the vulture; the rest of the herd are now very interested in this stranger in their midst and more of them start to walk towards it. The vulture tries its threat posture again, but this time it doesn't seem quite as convincing. The bird is nervous and, rather than staring at a single individual, it finds itself looking at maybe a dozen cows all getting closer and closer. The vulture steps backwards and then turns and performs what only can be described as an undignified waddle as it tries to put distance between itself and the cattle.

An inquisitive cow causing a Griffon Vulture to take evasive action.

The cows grow in confidence and with lowered heads start to increase their pace. The vulture with nervous looks behind, starts to stumble and then begins to jump through the grass; its movements becoming ever more frantic. It doesn't want to fly, it is full of food and it is also being forced to retreat up a slope, making it harder for the bird to take off. The increasing speed of the vulture's struggling withdrawal is a metaphorical red rag and the cows switch from a brisk trot to a run, their tails up once more and their heads down. I have never seen a vulture panic before, I wasn't sure that they could, but this bird certainly appears to be doing so as it bounds across the grass in clumsy hops and jumps, its legs propelling it along as it unfurls those large wings and begins to flap them in toilsome effort. With the cows closing in, the bird starts to get some lift, but the uphill terrain makes this a very long runway indeed and the charging cattle get uncomfortably near before, finally, the bird is able to break free from the ground, flapping its wings hard as it lifts itself up into the air. The cows don't seem to realise their quarry has departed though and, pumped full of excitement, the herd mentality reigns for several more seconds – more skittish dashes across the field, reliving the chase before eventually settling down once again.

I have often seen vultures clear up a cow, but have never before seen cows clear off a vulture.

The vanquished Griffon doesn't fly far, getting just enough height and momentum to be able to turn back around and fly over the stone wall before it lands back in amongst the others, settling down to loaf again, no doubt hoping it will finally be allowed to digest its meal in peace. I watch the field of vultures for a few more minutes as they sit within the green expanse against a backdrop of dehesa. Gradually their extended necks and heads lower as they relax into the renewed calmness. The cattle also watch them, blank stares across the stone wall, but gradually they lose interest in the birds and start to graze the grass in their own field.

I head back towards the village, ambling along for about half an hour before I get close to the first of the white-washed houses. I watch the newly arrived swallows skimming low over the fields at high speed and with low-flying agility whilst hawking the low-flying insects just centimetres above the green – a sure sign of rain according to weather folklore. Looking to the west, the truth in this belief seems proven as the clouds have thickened to a large, dark brooding mass. The loafing vultures, slowly digesting, will be disturbed again. They will notice the impending weather; they may sense the drop in air pressure or they may read the clouds, but either way they will want to be back at their roosting ledges to see the rain out.

In the evening, with the rain still falling, I look through many of the photos I have taken over the last few days – inevitably there are lots of photos of vultures. There is something I find fascinating about these birds and I am not sure what it is. I am a birdwatcher. I like birds. But vultures are something else. It could be their size – they are huge birds – but then so are the eagles and the Great Bustards they share this landscape with. Maybe it goes back to those Sunday night wildlife documentaries I watched as a child. Perhaps it is the way they look or is it because of their association with death and renewal? I don't really know why they have such a hold on me, but they do. They are special birds, and humans have long found them objects of fascination and veneration.

Vultures feature in the traditional beliefs of many human cultures – the ancient Egyptians saw them as a 'mother' figure and representations of these huge birds can be found in their written language, as well as in the decoration of treasures such as Tutankhamun's resplendent death mask. In South America, the American vultures, such as the condors, have also played a part in the traditional beliefs of the various nations. The Andean Condor, a huge vulture of the continent's mountainous spine, so large that it even dwarfs the Black Vulture of Europe, is still very much part of the culture of many of the continent's countries, and features on the flags of Bolivia and Ecuador, as well as appearing in the coats of arms of Chile and Colombia.

In North America, many of the Native American tribes have creation stories revolving around vultures, whilst on the Indian subcontinent the Hindu religion tells an epic tale of a noble vulture that engages in a heroic battle with a demon king despite knowing it will die. Even in Europe, vultures feature in many traditional tales. According to legend, Rome is situated where it is because the city's founders, Romulus and Remus, used vultures to determine the exact spot the city should be constructed on. They watched birds circling and took this as a sign that the location was ideal for their city. Of course, the vultures were probably circling on the thermals and updrafts created by the famous seven hills of Rome, but why spoil a good story.

Perhaps the most famous, or even infamous, human cultural tradition associated with vultures is that of the sky burial. The term sky burial refers to the deliberate exposure of a human corpse to scavenging birds. Sky burials were traditionally carried out by some followers of Buddhism and Zoroastrianism in countries including Tibet, China, Mongolia, Bhutan and parts of India. The practice still continues today, but is now quite rare, not only because of the marginalisation of religious practices such as this, but also because of the very real demise of the region's vulture population due to the Diclofenac poisoning, which wiped out ninety-nine per cent of these magnificent birds across large parts of the area where sky burials were once common place.

The male Blue Rock Thrush sings softly from atop his favourite rock, a deliberately selected place to sing his whistling melody and the already resplendent plumage rinsed through with the strong sunshine gives him an almost electric blue aura as he sings to impress his nearby, yet unseen, mate. He is a beautiful sight on a beautiful warm spring day but, as I watch him and enjoy his vibrancy, a metaphorical cloud appears that ominously threatens to end the calm tranquillity of this glorious day. A large coach has just pulled up on the side of the road, its engine thrumming loudly. I watch it warily from the corner of my eye as the thrum of the engine subsides, nothing happens for a few seconds and then the doors open with a loud release of pressured air. The coach disgorges its load, a noisy mass pours out from its innards – the Blue Rock Thrush goes quiet and then disappears, vanishing quickly from the scene.

School children fill the viewing areas. Across the river, the towering mass of igneous rock that is Peña Falcón basks in the early spring sunlight. The rock's large vulture colony

The beautiful Blue Rock Thrush is a bird capable of brightening up any landscape.

is its usual busy and active self, but the children don't see it; they are out of the confines of their classroom and able to evade the eye of their teachers. The noise they generate is incredible, reflecting and reverberating off the walls of stone around them – talking children, each one trying to be louder than the next. It is not great for Blue Rock Thrush watching, nor is it good for vulture watching and it is just impossible for the reverie of vulture gazing.

It is too much for me and I start to plan my escape, casting exaggerated looks of displeasure towards the Park staff that have, in my eyes at least, brought this invasion upon me. They try in vain to get the youngsters interested, try to get them one at a time to look through the telescope trained on the massive rock beyond. They don't appear interested; wildlife is not the topic of the children's conversation; instead, it is television, music and the latest fashion that are the dominant themes of the snatched chatter that I can hear.

Getting the next generation engaged with nature is vital if nature is going to survive, let alone flourish, in the future. Bringing them to the iconic Monfragüe National Park is, of course, a positive step, but a lack of discipline and an indifference on behalf of the teachers has turned this attempt into nothing more than an annoying farce. However, unseen by the noisy mass of youth and unseen by me, a Griffon Vulture makes a decision that dramatically changes the course of the school outing.

The decision is no more than a decision to step off the ledge it is on, to follow an air current that will take it up and away from the rocks, from the river, with the minimum of physical effort. It just so happens that the air current it enters initially flows below the eye line of those noisily standing at the viewing areas, before the orographical nature of the terrain pushes the highway of air through the valley's pinch point, shoving the current steeply upwards. The vulture has read this; it is why it has taken this route, and as the bird follows this aerial acclivity it appears, dramatically, just metres away from the gaggle of kids.

For seasoned vulture watchers like me, close encounters such as this are still awe-inspiring experiences; for a group of rowdy eleven-year-olds they are quite simply breathtaking. There is a shout and then, with surprising suddenness, a silence that is almost deafening in its intensity. None of the children make a sound. They appear to be physically unable to as they stand, open-mouthed, staring at the huge bird heading straight at them. The vulture isn't interested in the children, they are irrelevant to it, it is simply following the easiest route to altitude, it is only by chance that the route this bird is following takes the almost three-metre wingspan of the raptor right above their heads.

Pale head tucked in, outstretched wings held in a shallow V-shape, long primaries splayed like fingers, the vulture sails the current of air at speed. From where I am, I can hear the noise, the rush of sound created by those huge wings as they shear through the air. The children directly below the bird not only hear it, they feel it, some even duck involuntarily as the bird passes just a few metres over them.

That noise, that amazing noise, is the only sound to be heard. The bird banks right, following the air through the gap in the ridge, turning back towards the river and disappearing from view behind the pinnacle of rock known locally as the Salto de Gitano, Gypsy's leap. As the bird goes, so the noise of the children returns, but this time it is not their voices that echo off the rocks, it is a spontaneous round of applause. The Griffon is getting an ovation.

The ovation precedes an encore, the vulture spirals around again, flying over the children once more, but this time much higher and the climbing bird soars up through the air with ease. The hand-clapping slowly dies, replaced by pointing arms and the inevitable phones being held skywards. Wide-eyed, smiling children watching one of the world's biggest birds. As it gets further away, the audible murmur of excitement grows louder, the voices can be heard again, only this time the topic has changed.

I prefer to bird watch alone, to get lost with the birds. In most places I can do just that, but not here. This is one of the most popular birdwatching spots in the whole of the Iberian Peninsula, and for good reason too – it is spectacular. I move on, away from the children, but not as quickly as I had wanted to do a few moments earlier. Gone are my glowering looks, replaced by a more benign smile. Seeing a vulture fly so close is always spectacular; seeing the effect this bird had on the children is memorable. The unwitting bird has just tuned these youngsters into the world of wildlife in a way that the teachers and the Park's education staff couldn't do. The best thing for getting the next generation interested in the natural world is the natural world itself. As I walk back past the still-smiling, excited kids, I am mentally chastising myself for the initial cantankerousness I felt when they first arrived. They need to be here; I don't.

The future of vultures, the future of the vulture landscape, is dependent on our attitude towards these huge birds. Giving children the opportunity to experience these amazing birds up close and personal is vital if those children are going to grow up and respect them in the future. Without that respect, the space for vultures in our modern world becomes more and more pressurised. If we ignore them, ignore their relatively simple needs, then they will go. Forever.

MARCH

A vibrant palette of colour flanks the road, the wild spring flowers are in bloom and yellows, purples and whites dominate, interspersed with the occasional red of early Poppies. The scrub beyond the flowers is peppered with the white blooms of the Erezo, an endemic shrub closely related to Broom, a local symbol of spring that decorates the roadsides. At the quarry, the Spanish Sparrows are busy bickering amongst themselves in the spring sunshine. As I park the car in the shade of the quarry walls, I hear, over the sparrows' noisy argumentative chirps, the clear double syllable call of a more universal symbol of spring, a Common Cuckoo, announcing its return, a return that many of the small birds here won't be welcoming.

I look out over the water-filled quarry at the graceful Red-rumped Swallows gliding slowly over it, mesmerised by their movements. I watch these hirundine distractions for a few seconds before my eyes are inevitably drawn to the terraced sheer faces of blasted rock opposite me. I can see several Griffon Vultures dotted about them. There are more in the sky, but it is the ones that are hunkered down on the ledges that I want to have a close look at. I set up the tripod and attach the telescope. As I do so, one of the male Spanish Sparrows lands on the railings by me, looking curiously at my actions before deciding the hustle and bustle of the flock is much more interesting.

I bend to peer through the telescope and the first bird I see is not a large vulture, but a humbug-headed Rock Bunting with a beak full of straggly grasses that immediately disappears into a crevice, evidently constructing its nest within. Above it, a more obvious nest sits on a rocky ledge, a large jumbled collection of sticks, improbably compiled into a coherent structure. A Griffon Vulture sits tight across its top, gazing blankly at the activities of the many small passerines around it. The bird sits there motionless, offering me no indication of what is going on beneath – has the egg hatched yet, is there new life keeping warm under the mass of feathers of its parent? I keep the telescope trained on the nest and look about me with my naked eye.

Fresh sticks have been placed on the scruffy Egyptian Vulture's nest above me, but the bird is nowhere to be seen. It won't be long, however, before the female lays her eggs within it, perhaps even just a few days from now. A male Blue Rock Thrush sings happily from the top of the rocks, basking in the sunlight whilst performing his pleasing melody. Several male Serin, beautifully bright, are rattling off their silvery tune, proclaiming their territories from their various vantage points. The Red-rumped Swallows have now landed at the edge of the water and are gathering up mud to add to their tunnelled structures slung

Humbug-headed Rock Buntings can often be found near to where Griffon Vultures breed.

under a nearby rock overhang. A Hoopoe starts to perform, dropping its head downwards, creating a double-chinned profile from which its namesake song resounds.

At least two Black Redstarts are singing, competing against each other and striving to sound the most impressive, whilst gangs of Spotless Starlings roam the wide grass-topped tiers of the quarry's sides in constant conversation with one another. It is a concert of bird sound, amplified and concentrated by the bowl and its reflective rock walls, a multi-headlined musical extravaganza with all the acts performing at the same time.

Above the aural performance, a couple of overhead vultures circle the quarry, losing altitude. I glance at the bird sitting on the nest through the telescope and, sure enough, it has seen them, neck stretched upwards, watching intently. One of the descending birds is preparing to land on the ledge next to the nest. Legs down, wings splayed out, it drops below the level of the ledge before rising up to it at the last moment, landing perfectly by its mate. Strange hisses and hoarse grunts emanate from the pair as they greet each other. The bird on the nest tentatively gets up, looks beneath itself and then waddles off the nest.

A small, white downy head pops up above the tangled mass of sticks before collapsing back down again, the neck muscles too weak and uncoordinated to hold the weight of the disproportionately massive head for long. The newly arrived adult shuffles carefully into the nest, looking down bemusedly at the young helpless chick within. The chick tries to raise its head once more, but the adult puts a stop to it by gently lowering itself down over

The large wedge-shaped tail and the small pointed head of the Egyptian Vulture give it a distinctive shape.

the top of small downy parcel of life, enveloping the newly hatched young vulture in its warm feathers.

In the following hour, the scene is repeated several times throughout the colony, the angular quarry walls home to many examples of new vulture life. Incubation duties over, the relieved Griffons shuffle along the ledges, look about themselves, look out into the quarry, look up at the open air above them and then step off into freedom.

After an hour of vulture watching and gazing, I rouse myself into movement. I walk back past the car, leaving it nestled in the shade and head out of the confines of the quarry, picking my way gingerly over the cattle grid as I go. A Sardinian Warbler sits on an exposed branch, black head and red eye showing as it scolds me for daring to be there, Azure-winged Magpies call to themselves as they flit across the track in front of me and several Spotless Starlings, at their shiniest best, flash by in a tight little group. The distinctive black and white shape of an adult Egyptian Vulture catches my eye as I scan the sky above me, its white wedge of a tail and sharp contrast of the black and white underwings give this vulture a smart appearance; it looks good. But does it think it needs something more, perhaps a bit of cosmetic improvement?

Avian cosmetics is a term that has been coined to describe the practice of birds adorning themselves in material to change their appearance; in other words, birds that wear make-up. This is behaviour that can't be explained by a need for camouflage, nor is it a behaviour that seems to confer any health benefits; it just appears to be simply cosmetic. The occurrence of avian cosmetics in the bird world is a very rare one. There are around nine and a half thousand species of bird, but only a dozen of them are known to apply materials cosmetically. Two of these are vultures.

It seems that the Egyptian and the Bearded Vultures like to put on a bit of rouge every now and then to enhance their appearance. They like to apply a red-brown tinge to their plumage, selecting iron-rich pools and puddles of muddy water in which to bathe. Studies have shown that these two vulture species choose the coloured puddles over clear water ones and then go through a deliberate process of anointing the red-brown liquid onto parts of their plumage, staining it as they do so.

It appears that the birds exhibiting this behaviour tend to be dominant adults and it is therefore thought that the application of cosmetics is a way in which the individual bird can inform others of its high status. Little is known of this practice and no one is really sure what it signifies, but it does illustrate how much we still have to learn about birds, even big obvious ones such as vultures that have been comparatively well studied. The Egyptian above me though is immaculate in its plumage – no make-up has been applied to this vulture.

There is some red in the landscape, however, as several Poppy flowers, improbably supported on their lanky stems and ahead of schedule, dot the track edge as it meanders through the scrubby dehesa. The red heads of Woodchat Shrikes become more numerous each day, as these small predators continue to return from their wintering grounds, staking out their territories on arrival, several have caught my eye since I left the quarry, making short flights on their black and white wings between the trees. Their bigger congener, the Iberian Grey Shrike is taking a more leisurely approach, sitting on an old redundant telegraph pole and using the leaning vantage point to scour the ground below.

Above me, five Griffon Vultures sweep past, one after the other, following the same aerial highway back to the quarry. I follow their lead and head back too, only at a much slower pace. In the time it takes me to walk ten metres, they are already within the walls of the quarry. Once there, I look at the beginnings of a new generation of vultures, at the adults sitting protectively over their tiny charges, before I gather up my telescope and tripod, get in to the car and head back down the winding road in to the Tajo valley.

The red head of the Woodchat Shrike is a real eyecatcher in the spring.

I stop at the impressive Roman bridge that spans the river, linking both banks today just as it has done for almost two thousand years. Its resident Blue Rock Thrush sits proudly atop the grand triumphal arch in the centre, its Roman nose of a beak silhouetted on top of the Roman statement against the bright sky behind it. I wonder how many of its ancestors have held this lofty architectural territory before it, using the historical structure as a nesting cliff. Crag Martins buzz the sun-lit wall below me, following regular circuits along it, hawking insects attracted by the radiated warmth with jinking flight, flashing mirrors and impossible turns. Under the central arches, above the turgid non-flowing river, hundreds of House Martins nests are busy with birds. Amongst these white-rumped martins are several House Sparrows, quickly stuffing stolen nests with grasses, claiming them as their own and aggressively repelling any attempts at eviction by the rightful owners.

A sudden outbreak of panic under the middle arch causes sparrows and martins to abandon their fractious nesting activity, calling sharply in alarm, taking flight and heading downstream as a Black Kite glides menacingly through the arch – the ultimate avian opportunist has returned from its winter quarters. Composure restored, the martins switch on their flight skills and mob the much bigger, but much less agile predator, driving it away from their nesting area. The kite speeds up its glide with a subtle change of wing angle and moves on, leaving the anger it created behind. But it will be back, the abundance of nesting birds in the arch is too much for this bird to ignore.

The first Black Kite of the year always means something to me, their return is my symbol of spring, coinciding as it does with the beginning of another year in my life. I celebrate my birthday with Black Kites. I look skyward and see three more distinctive dark shapes spread out across the sky. There were no Black Kites to be seen this morning as I drove here through prime kite territories; they were still travelling, making their way back to their breeding grounds in this vulture landscape. Within days they will be everywhere, over the river valleys, over the plains, the dehesas and the towns, always on the lookout for opportunities to obtain a meal, no matter how big or how small. Their presence will have been noted by the vultures, their activities will now be watched, their behaviour read, interpreted and relayed through the visibility chains. Black Kites are the unwitting scouts of the vultures.

After the bridge, I wind back up the other side of the valley, heading into the town. A male Serin sits atop the traffic light that guards the pedestrian crossing, its colour much brighter than the jaded signal. Heading out through the town, I see dozens of hirundines dashing about the houses, busily flying over the road, chasing down insects and pursuing rivals.

I take the track across the plains. Larks everywhere are singing their beautiful songs from fence posts or in fluttering flight above, sometimes dashing along the track edges, other times amongst the flowers and grasses. A group of male Great Bustards strut majestically, heads held high on powerful-looking necks, the soft grey of the head blending down the neck into a belt of bright chestnut. They look at me with suspicion, huge, heavy, spectacular-looking birds, their bristle-like chin feathers adding to their air of superiority. They turn and walk away from me, still strutting, but at a faster pace. They use the undulations of the plain to remove themselves from my view.

The males are gathering now, grouping together at long-used traditional sites, their immaculate plumage at its very best as they prepare for the lek, the annual contest to impress the females.

A cloud of white grows out of nothing in one of the fields further off. A look through the binoculars confirms it as a male Great Bustard, the normally subtle plumage transformed into a foaming bath of white extravagance. Head tucked in, plumage turned inside out showing all the loose white feathers that normally remain tucked away. This mass of white shakes adding to the spectacle. He is putting on a show and, looking to the right, I see his audience, the object of his desires – a female, so much smaller than the bulking males, so much more subdued in plumage; there is no flamboyance or strutting from her. There is also no interest in the male, despite his best efforts. The female completely ignores the shimmering white show off in front of her as she, head down, searches for the small seeds she feeds on.

There is more white showing in the huge expanse of fenced grass – an adult Egyptian Vulture is using its long thin bill to pull hard at something on the ground, grasping it with its feet, pulling against its grip, trying to tear whatever it is into more manageable pieces. Through the binoculars I see the effort in its yolk-yellow face, the head twisting and turning, trying to rend the dirt-encrusted object.

A Black Kite ghosts in, flying over the scene and looking intently at what the bigger bird is doing. It sees an opportunity and lands nearby, shuffling in on foot towards the vulture, but the Egyptian is not for sharing. It drops the potential food, lowers its head and opens its wings in a gesture clearly aimed at the kite, unequivocally demonstrating which of them is the biggest. The kite takes heed of the threat, stopping and turning to the side before slowly walking a few yards away. But it doesn't fly away; it stays where it is, watching the vulture return to its task with interest. The vulture tries another angle, showing the kite its back as it desperately tries to rip whatever it is it is holding in its talons.

The vulture's luck isn't in – first the kite and now two Ravens. The black corvids wheel in on outstretched wings, cronking harshly at the scene below; not for them the hesitant approach of the kite, no, the pair head straight for

An Egyptian Vulture in flight; the small, relatively weak bill is clearly visible.

the vulture, aiming to land virtually on top of it. This time the Egyptian doesn't put up a defence, the Ravens are the smallest of the three birds, although only just, but they are evidently the most formidable. Grabbing its find in its beak, the Egyptian jumps into the air, unfolding its long broad wings, flapping them hard as it flies off low over the field. The object in the bird's bill appears to be a mangled, dirty piece of afterbirth, perhaps from the field of sheep and newborn lambs to the right of where this drama has been playing out.

The Ravens are not going to allow the vulture to get away; they are quickly after it, calling loudly, harassing it from behind, grabbing at its tail feathers with their menacing bills. The kite doesn't follow; instead it shuffles over to the area of flattened grass where the vulture had been struggling in vain, it looks intently at the ground but fails to find anything. Overhead, and coming from different directions, two Griffon Vultures drift by, no doubt attracted by the actions of the other three species, but they see nothing other than the disappointed kite and so continue to effortlessly drift across the sky. I gaze at the Griffons for a minute or two, watching them scanning the plains below them, reading the signs, ready to investigate potential opportunities.

I find the Egyptian Vulture again, but it is no longer flying, it is standing forlornly in a field, a victim of piracy. I follow its gaze and see the two Ravens, jet black heads in a sea of grasses looking about them guardedly before dipping down below to feed on their booty.

I leave the piratical corvids and the disappointed vulture and move onwards. Crested and Calandra Larks squat as I approach before flying up from right in front of me as I drive down the track leaving a faint mist of dust to hang in the air behind me. I stop at the point the track begins to descend back to the tarmac road – a vista of openness runs away in front of me to the distant hills with Portugal on the western horizon framing the picture.

Vultures are dominant in the sky, a far-off circling mass of them towards the Tajo valley is disbanding. Individual Griffons are at all points of the aerial compass, and amongst them I see four Black Vultures, their flatter wings in comparison to the Griffons obvious as I watch them all float through the sky. A Zitting Cisticola, a dark bouncing dot against the bright sky, performs its song flight, a high-frequency 'zitt' accompanying each exaggerated undulation of the bird's flight. It lands on some barbed wire on the other side of the track, the sunlight picking out the rich stripy markings of this otherwise small brown bird.

Alarm calls catch my ear and I spot some agitated Corn Buntings and larks over the grass field to my right. The cause of their alarm is a fox, the canid trotting through the green sea of grass stems, ignoring the birds' cries of disapproval. It pauses to look at my figure on its horizon, an inquisitive head staring at me, assessing my threat level before it moves on, adjusting the angle of its route across the grasses to maintain its distance. The orange-red of the fur on its back looks soft and luxurious in the sunlight.

It disappears into a fold of land, one of the many creases in the grassy fabric of the plain's landscape, its unseen route still followable thanks to the unending supply of small birds that take umbrage at the predator's presence. It reappears towards the wire netting fence that separates the grass from a field of long turned-over stubble, a mass of broken clods of earth with lines etched in them from last year's plough still about visible. The expanse of brown soil is broken here and there by irregular circles of green, varying sizes of grassy patches, delineating where the geological dog's teeth are lurking. The fox follows the fence line for about twenty metres before dipping down and slipping under it with vulpine suppleness, trotting onwards across the exposed soil before eventually vanishing from my view.

I might not be able to see the fox anymore, but others have – a flock of nine previously hidden Black-bellied Sandgrouse take to the air in a simultaneous flash of their eponymous black bellies and white wings; the fox's presence evidently too close for comfort for these ground dwellers. Their beautiful bubbling flight calls drift across the plains as they fly furiously, banking away from the field before arcing back into the far end of it. The eye-catching black and white of the flying birds disappears as they fold their wings and land amongst the clods of soil and faint plough lines, blending in with their background seamlessly. I watch over the plain for a few more minutes, watching the busy activity of the larks and buntings, and I lapse into some vulture gazing as a Griffon flies directly overhead, its head turning side to side as it observes what is happening in its three-dimensional space. A farm vehicle, trailing dust, moves me back into the now as it heads up the hill towards me. I get back in the car, exchange a greeting with the other vehicle's driver and head off down to the tarmac road. I have one more stop to make before I head home.

The Salor valley is alive with the sounds of birds. Chaffinches sing loudly, their descending notes mixing with the more discordant jabber of the Spanish Sparrows; softer voices can be picked out – a Rock Bunting is singing somewhere nearby; and further away is the melodic warble of a Blackbird floating in the air. In the twisted, scrubby oaks that pepper the upper slopes of the valley, Common Cuckoos are calling out their name, accompanied by the occasional harsh screech of a Jay.

I walk down the angled track, the air above me thick with House Martins and Crag Martins. Both species are intent on nest building and are gathering mud in their beaks to plaster onto the bridge structures behind me. In front of me, where a small tributary meets the river, a muddy-edged pool has formed and clouds of martins are there, some descending, some rising, others gathering. It is a hectic hive of activity and the birds coming down have to hover on a blur of wings as they try to find enough space in which to land amidst the other birds already gathering up the precious mud.

The vultures are up; a couple of Blacks are following the course of the valley downstream, gliding through the air on their flat wings, using the movement of the air to carry them along. There are several Griffons across the sky, a sky that resembles a painting with delicate brush strokes of wispy clouds across a blue canvas.

A ring of ripples expanding across the turgid surface of the water draws my attention – something has slipped in from one of the rocks that push out of the water. I dismiss it as nothing more than a terrapin, more of which I see sunbathing on the various rocks along the riverside, but as I am dismissing it, bubbles appear from below, tracing a route across the surface, rapidly becoming a straight line heading diagonally away from me. I watch this ephemeral line transfixed, I think I know the cause, but am unsure. Can I really be that lucky?

I am. The source appears, an Otter breaks the surface of the still water, her head turns to look at me and for a brief couple of glorious seconds I find myself in a staring contest with this marvellous mustelid. It doesn't last long; she dives and is gone, her thick tail disappearing behind her. I spend several minutes scanning the river, trying to see her again, hoping to see her again, but to no avail. She's gone, but the memory will live forever.

A Kingfisher blazes past in a bolt of electric blue, the vibrancy of the plumage and the loud sharp call it gives as it bullets past me jolts me from my Otter-inspired reverie. After the burning blue sear fades from my eyes, a flash of white catches my attention. A male Black Wheatear on the opposite side of the river perches on one of the rounded rocks at the bottom of the large stack of boulders that reinforce the sheer face of rock on which the main road above has its foundations. The small matt black bird sings its high-pitched faint song, pumping its tail vigorously, signalling its presence before flying away up the slope and flashing the white rump and tail as it goes in blatant advertisement. It lands on a thin crumbly outcrop of layered rock from where it sings again, combining its thin voice with yet more territorial tail pumping. Down at the water's edge is another pumping tail, but this time it's a Common Sandpiper. Another combination of light and dark, but this is

The beautiful valley of the Rio Salor.

brown and white, the dainty wader bobs its rear end as it picks its way around the stones on the water's edge, its immaculate white underside reflecting back at it from the still bay of water.

I stand for a moment on the stony beach that has been formed on the inside of the river's meandering curve. The sun's warmth reflects back up at me from the flat, rounded stones at my feet, all angular edges smoothed away by millennia of water flow. The rich silt deposited between the stones by the winter spate already colonised by a mass of different green stems, all racing upwards towards the sun, whilst the roots below secure themselves in this temporary landscape.

A large torn-off bough of an oak lies stranded at the point where the disc-like stones give way to more permanent grasses. Deposited at the water's peak, the bough is already over ten metres from where the water now lies, abandoned by the river that carried it along. The broken bark is alive with insects, beetles scurry across it, large ants forage its many cracks and crevices, whilst flies use its elevated position to bask in the sunlight.

Somewhere in the valley I hear the faint sound of stock bells, but the animals remain out of sight as their movements are relayed through the air in soft metallic peals. A Black Stork flies over the river, a black and white pattern against the azure blue sky. It is following the watercourse and using the flow of air to carry it along. It enters a thermal, wheeling around in exaggerated circles using the motion of the air generated by the reflected heat to gain the height it needs to exit the valley. Every turn it makes in the sunlight changes the black feathers on its head and neck into iridescent shades of violet and green. The Kingfisher pipes its return, a blur of blue zipping over the stones, taking the direct route rather than following the wandering river, a straight-line dash that continues back over the water, a bright tracer standing out against the darkness of the water below it. Eventually it perches on a low branch that sticks out above the water, a momentary pause giving me a brief glimpse of its beautiful red-orange front, before it is off again, flying low, fast and straight, heading further up the river and out of sight.

I follow the colourful fish eater upstream, walking along the grassy banks and scrambling over the rocky interruptions, pausing to enjoy the valley, to listen to the bird song and to watch the vultures overhead. I find a suitable rocky seat, a large split boulder with a smooth flat surface that is perfect to sit on. From my elevated position I can look over two stretches of open water separated from one another by a narrow shallow section where the river is constricted by the pinch of a narrow rocky line that runs across the valley. A Heron, head back in its shoulders, its dagger-like bill tucked into the fluff of feathers on its chest, stands on a rock in the middle of the open water on my left. It is absolutely motionless and takes the opportunity for an afternoon nap in the gentle spring warmth. At the far end of the water, one of its relatives, a pure white Little Egret is busy stalking the shallows, refusing the temptations of the siesta as it hunts for a meal. As I scan back along the water's edge I catch up again with the colours of the Kingfisher, perched motionless on an exposed tree root that juts out horizontally from the eroded bank like an accusing finger. The bird's dark, dagger-like bill points downwards, the eyes follow its direction intently, staring beyond and into the dark water, waiting. It sits motionless, a small blob of blue in a setting of greens and browns.

For a minute or two, all that moves are a few leaves above the bird, tickled by the air moving idly by. Then, all action, the dark dagger drops vertically, a blur of blue follows, a splash of water, droplets thrown upwards, mini rainbows cascading back to the river and, as they fall, the blue and orange of the bird rises through them, landing back on the accusatory finger it started from. It was all so quick that it is hard to comprehend. The Kingfisher is exactly where it was before, but this time the dagger isn't pointing downwards – it is holding a small fish.

The dagger is transformed into a dextrous digit as the small fish is expertly manoeuvred. A Bee-eater-like snap of the head, a whack against the branch and the king of fishers subdues its quarry. More manoeuvring lines the fish up and it is quickly swallowed head first. A quick shimmy, a ruffle of feathers and then the bird leaves the finger-like perch once

more, but this time in a horizontal motion, flying bullet straight along the water, piping its call as it exits the scene.

The somewhat tuneless tong-tong-tong noise of the stock bells increases noticeably and, looking behind me, I spot a small herd of goats making their way through the Cistus scrub. A semi-nomadic capricious group, there are a dozen or so of them, ringing their way along the valley, the bells to help their owners find them when needed. They browse briefly at everything, trying all in their quest for sustenance. The lead goat stops and eyes me for a moment, shakes a fly off its head and continues its way, the others following behind, uninterested in my presence. A sharp acrid scent precedes them and hangs in the air after they have passed, eventually fading with the sound of their collar bells.

A Black Vulture drifts by high overhead, whilst the dry clicks of House Martins fill the air as they swoop and dash acrobatically, harvesting the bountiful mass of flying insects. Frogs chorus, unseen crickets stridulate loudly and lizards scurry noisily through the vegetation, a surround sound experience.

The clouds have often promised much, but they have failed to deliver on their potential. The rains of March never materialised, the land is dry, the water in the many stock ponds dotted across this landscape evaporates a bit more every day. The rivers still flow, but only just, as if the effort of motion is too much for them. It is going to be a hard year. The Extremeños have seen it all before. They have a saying for times like this: "*Sera un buen año por los buitres*" – it will be a good year for the vultures.

A breeze of air flows down the valley faster than the languid water below, creating eddies of movement for the Griffon Vultures above. The valley meanders its way through the landscape, its curves emphasising the enveloping beauty of the place. This is indeed a vulture landscape, but as I stand here feeling the breeze, inhaling the aromas, hearing the sounds of nature all around me, I realise, as I look up at a circling Griffon, that it is also mine.

APPENDICES

VULTURES OF THE WORLD

Vultures are found right across the globe and their native ranges include every continent apart from Australia and Antarctica.

Old World Vultures (16 species)

Common name	Scientific name	Distribution	Global status*
Bearded Vulture	*Gypaetus barbatus*	Europe, Africa, Asia	Near Threatened
Palm-nut Vulture	*Gypohierax angolensis*	Africa	Least Concern
Egyptian Vulture	*Neophron percnopterus*	Europe, Africa, Asia	Endangered
Black Vulture	*Aegypius monachus*	Europe, Asia	Near Threatened
Griffon Vulture	*Gyps fulvus*	Europe, Africa, Asia	Least Concern
White-rumped Vulture	*Gyps bengalensis*	Asia	Critically Endangered
Rüppell's Vulture	*Gyps rueppelli*	Africa	Critically Endangered
Indian Vulture	*Gyps indicus*	Asia	Critically Endangered
Slender-billed Vulture	*Gyps tenuirostris*	Asia	Critically Endangered
Himalayan Vulture	*Gyps himalayensis*	Asia	Near Threatened
White-backed Vulture	*Gyps africanus*	Africa	Critically Endangered
Cape Vulture	*Gyps coprotheres*	Africa	Endangered
Hooded Vulture	*Necrosyrtes monachus*	Africa	Critically Endangered
Red-headed Vulture	*Sarcogyps calvus*	Asia	Critically Endangered
Lappet-faced Vulture	*Torgos tracheliotos*	Africa, Asia	Endangered
White-headed Vulture	*Trigonoceps occipitalis*	Africa	Critically Endangered

* IUCN (2019). The IUCN Red List of Threatened Species. Version 2019-3. http://www.iucnredlist.org (accessed 10 December 2019).

New World Vultures (7 species)

Common name	Scientific name	Distribution (Americas)	Global status*
Black Vulture	*Coragyps atratus*	South, Central, North	Least Concern
Turkey Vulture	*Cathartes aura*	South, Central, North	Least Concern
Lesser Yellow-headed Vulture	*Cathartes burrovianus*	South, Central	Least Concern
Greater Yellow-headed Vulture	*Cathartes melambrotus*	South	Least Concern
California Condor	*Gymnogyps californianus*	North	Critically Endangered
Andean Condor	*Vultur gryphus*	South	Near Threatened
King Vulture	*Sarcoramphus papa*	South, Central	Least Concern

* IUCN (2019). The IUCN Red List of Threatened Species. Version 2019-3. http://www.iucnredlist.org (accessed 10 December 2019).

You will notice that a Black Vulture is listed in both the Old World and the New World birds; however, they are completely different species despite both being black in colour, hence their shared common name. To try and avoid confusion, alternative names have been suggested, with the common-sense suggestion of appending the two names with either European or American being the most straightforward. Unfortunately, common sense doesn't always prevail, and the Black Vulture of Europe and the vulture landscape has now been officially renamed as the Cinereous Vulture. Cinereous means ash grey – but the Black Vulture of Europe is not ash grey, it is black. Unsurprisingly, this renaming has caused further confusion and some controversy, with many ornithologists and birdwatchers, including me, continuing to use the old, properly descriptive name.

EXTREMADURA – THE VULTURE LANDSCAPE

Extremadura is one of fifteen autonomous communities that make up mainland Spain. It is in the central west of the country, forming part of the national border with neighbouring Portugal and is a large region, over twice the size of Wales, but with only just over a million people living in it (Wales has just over three million). The region's administrative centre is in the old Roman capital of the area, Merida, with the region being further split into two provinces: Cáceres in the north and Badajoz in the south.

The main industry is agriculture, but the hot dry climate of the summer months and the rocky terrain of many parts has meant that the agriculture here has always been very extensive in practice. It is an under-populated region and, even today, its inhabitants are migrating away from the rural life to other parts of Spain and the rest of the world. However, this is not a new phenomenon – many of Spain's historic explorers and conquistadors came from the region before heading off to seek glory and wealth in other parts of the world.

Today, tourism plays a big part in the region's economy. There are many fantastic historical sights, from Roman artefacts and buildings through to the sumptuous palaces and squares built from the wealth of Spain's old empire. Wildlife is also a big draw for many visitors, especially those from other parts of Europe. Some of the continent's rarest wildlife can be found in Extremadura. The vultures are joined by five species of eagle, two bustard species and, slowly but surely, a returning population of one of the rarest mammals in the world, the Iberian Lynx.